MOMENTS
THAT
MADE
THE
MOVIES

MOMENTS
THAT MADE THE
MOVIES

DAVID THOMSON

With 250 Illustrations

Thames & Hudson

In illustrating this book, whenever possible we have shown the actual moment being described. Occasionally that has resulted in a selection that may not be as perfectly polished or illumined as one might expect, but that—we hope— catches the pulse of the moment in question. —The Editors

First published in hardcover in the United States of America in 2013 by Thames & Hudson Inc., 500 Fifth Avenue, New York, NY 10110 thamesandhudsonusa.com

ISBN: 978-0-500-51641-6

LIBRARY OF CONGRESS CATALOGUE CARD NUMBER: 2012952804

Printed in China

for Mary Corliss, Lucy Gray and Molly Haskell

CONTENTS

INTRODUCTION

Do you remember the movies you saw, like whole vessels serene on the seas of time? Or do you just retain moments from them, like shattered lifeboats where a very fierce tiger and Hedy Lamarr (change the animals to fit your history) are gazing at you from the other end of the boat wondering how the story will end? Can you recall the intricate plot of *Laura*, or do you simply see Dana Andrews falling asleep beneath that portrait on the wall? Most people, I find, remember moments from films they saw as children or adolescents (so true film buffs like to extend those stages of life). Yet often the moment has overwhelmed the film itself.

At fifteen, I walked into *Rebel Without a Cause* before the end of the previous screening, and I was confronted by the scene in which James Dean is trying to coax Sal Mineo (and his gun) out of the planetarium. In the movie as a whole, Jim (Dean) is as kind to Plato (Mineo) as an older brother and is trying to save him. But in that first moment, I saw Dean making a plan: so he seemed devious and cunning, and I always have seen his character, Jim Stark, as less a lost kid than a potential director.

If we conform to the ancient tradition of twenty-four frames in a movie second, then a two-hour film has 172,800 frames. It's a stretch to regard every frame as a moment, but fifteen frames can make a distinct contribution to and shift in a film, while some other moments last a minute or two, or even twenty minutes. There are certain films—like *High Noon* or *12 Angry Men*—where the entire picture may be construed as an extended moment, a piece of unbroken duration, and a kind of narrative momentousness. I noticed, as I composed this book, that some films seemed packed with distinct, quotable moments, while others—often great works—seemed to possess a continuity from which it was more difficult to isolate or extract moments. Once you were into that sort of film, it was harder to get out. Jean Renoir's movies—*La Règle du Jeu* especially—seem to flow like the rivers he often took as a model. It is harder with Renoir to attend to just one scene without wanting to speak about everything in the film. Yet American films, by and large, do look to have sensational events, knock-out set-pieces that will be treasured long after the rest is forgotten and which will feature in the trailers and the advertisements.

I have already mentioned a few films, like *La Règle du Jeu* and *High Noon*, that I did not select for this book. Of course, most of the films ever made are not in the book, and I hasten to distance myself from any attempt by publishers,

OPPOSITE: *Gene Tierney in her* Laura *mood, but in a moment not* in the film. *Is this actually a publicity still (she's holding the crucial gun)?*

9

reviewers, or readers to claim that these choices are the "best" moments in the history of movies, or even my personal favorites. That is not the case. But these are moments that have stayed in my memory, and which leap onto the screen in my head if the title is mentioned. I think they are very "movie" moments, doing something that could be managed in no other medium—the look, the pace, the movement, the texture, the context, all these things are vital. I can describe them, or I will try, but really you have to witness them and feel them.

I was excited by the challenge to write about them, but I hope the moments will send you in search of the whole films, especially those you had never heard of, or not seen before. There are surprises, offbeat choices, perhaps even capricious or provocative selections, as well as plenty of films that you might have guessed would be included—though not always with the moments you anticipated.

You see, there is a gentle theory at work in this book, which is to wonder, "Well, what is a movie moment?" and in turn that may lead readers into the larger question of how movies function as stories, dreams, and shows, and how they become as potent in our imaginations as the rooms in which we spent our childhood. As you go along, reading and looking in whatever order seems most persuasive, I hope you will begin to think about the special nature of film, how these dreams are made, and the fascinating but fragile friendship between writing and film.

Finally, there can only be so many moments in this book. You would have to count them to discover just how many. And whatever the number is it could easily have been doubled, or multiplied by ten. Once you start to see moments, you become like an editor or a director, getting closer to the strange dreamlike reality of movies. Don't be troubled about what is left out. The selection is, of course, personal. If I ask you, "Did you enjoy your dinner last night?" you don't think of replying, "Well, there was no omelet, no halibut, no pheasant, no beef, no pasta, no figs stuffed with sweetbreads, not a sight of a persimmon pudding, and not so much as a mention of a decent vindaloo or a pomegranate sorbet." Instead, you say, "We had a rack of lamb with fingerling potatoes, spinach merely shown hot water, and parsnips roasted in thyme and rosemary, followed by fresh peaches—and we liked it." This is a book about what has been offered, and the table is spread for your pleasure. Don't let your immense experience of cuisine spoil the meal.

I suspect this menu of moments—and your own when you get around to compiling it—will take you back to your childhood—both the one you actually had and the one you longed for under the inspiration of those great, glowing dreams and the dark they rely on.

Liz Taylor—
I'll have what
she's having.

MOMENTS
THAT
MADE
THE
MOVIES

ONE WOMAN STANDING, ANOTHER SITTING AND CROSSING LEGS

1887, EADWEARD MUYBRIDGE

Animal Locomotion

The one thing popular history recalls is that Muybridge helped settle a bet: whether in its galloping stride, there were instants when a horse had all its feet off the ground. But the great bulk of his intensely beautiful work has no sort of gaming instinct in its heart. He wants us to look at the thing he called "Animal Locomotion" for its own sake, and for ours, and he wanted us to learn to rejoice in what was a barely appreciated phenomenon of democracy— for instance, that just about everyone could sit down. It was a right and a glory.

And I do mean *barely*. It may be that working at a university (Pennsylvania) and requiring its funds, he was obliged to take a scientific, physiological approach in which it was understood that human motion, to be most fully described, required nakedness in the subjects. After all, the horse had been nude. It was also possible that work-study students at the university in the very up-to-date late 1880s were unusually accommodating about taking off their clothes. They do seem fairly happy in their work. But as you leaf through the volumes of *Animal Locomotion*, it becomes clear that Muybridge was as much in ecstasy over the human body as George Stubbs had been with horses in the eighteenth century.

The series I have chosen, out of hundreds, is of two women, in what I take to be their early twenties. (There are just as many series with men, and I must warn you that in both genres there is no coyness about private organs or pubic hair, though over seventy years later such matters would have been taken to court.)

In this series, one woman wears a bracelet. Apart from that they are naked, and they are not unattractive. There are eight pictures in the series, and the action is as follows: One girl, with shorter, lighter hair, holds a plain wooden chair ready as another woman with darker, longer hair prepares to sit in the chair. She turns and dips her bottom toward the platform of the chair. The standing woman braces her left leg slightly to support the small force in the act of sitting. The darker woman sits back in the chair and continues to smoke—she has had a cigarette in her left hand all the time. And the standing woman bends her left leg back, less in an engineering move than in sheer instinct or pleasure, and dips her head down over the head of the sitting woman so that they may talk together more intimately.

OPPOSITE:
The photographer's name was Eadweard Muybridge; the ladies are unknown. It was an experiment in optics, but anyone could feel the erotic prospect of holding such pictures in your hand.

13

" …there is an amity between them, a sympathy that pays no attention to the process of being photographed."

The atoms of time, the frames of a movie, and maybe the first chorus line of the new age? At the University of Pennsylvania, work study students model for Muybridge.

We do not know their names—or at least I do not—so I am inclined to think of them as Celine and Julie. For there is an amity between them, a sympathy that pays no attention to the process of being photographed or the grid marks on the wall behind them that are a feature of so many Muybridge photographs. (I should add that this place is in the open—we can feel the sunlight on the bodies and the film's silver.)

There are two other sets in the series, both of eight pictures, one taken from the rear of the standing woman, though at an angle, and the other from in front of the two women. The harmony of the three sets is very pleasing,

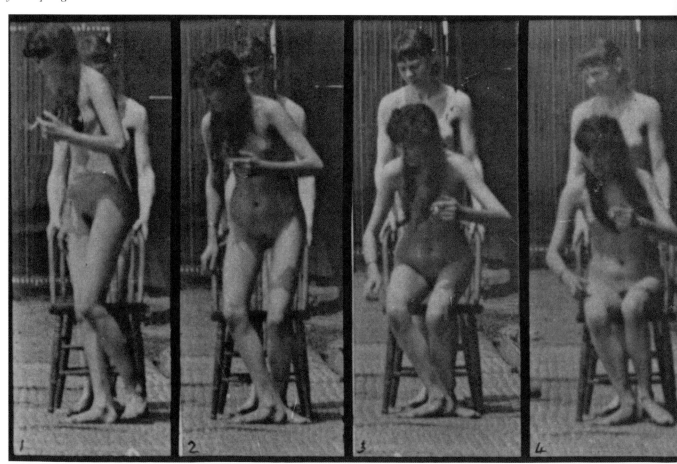

and it may be instructive from an anatomist's point of view, but the most pressing point about the threesome is the realization that there will probably have to be crosscutting or editing.

This is not movie, yet it is a series of sequential stills, and that is one way of defining the process of movie. In what it shows, and in the natural intimacy—the easeful rapport—that exists between the two women, this is decades ahead of the tenor of most movies in the forty or so years that would follow. When you look at Muybridge you truly feel the calm revolution in the making—the sight of human action and the plain proof that time is passing. These are great, tiny movies, so lucid, so luminous, and so ordinary that you wonder why anyone really bothered with the whole circus of making movies. It's 1887 and it's obvious: We are having such fun as time passes. That's what we hardly knew before—it wasn't just the horse; we were flying, too.

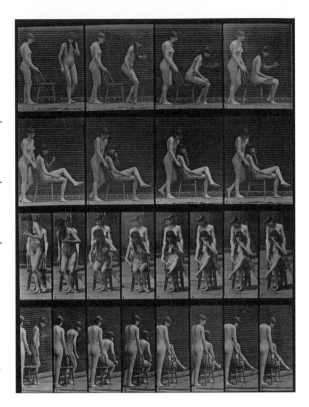

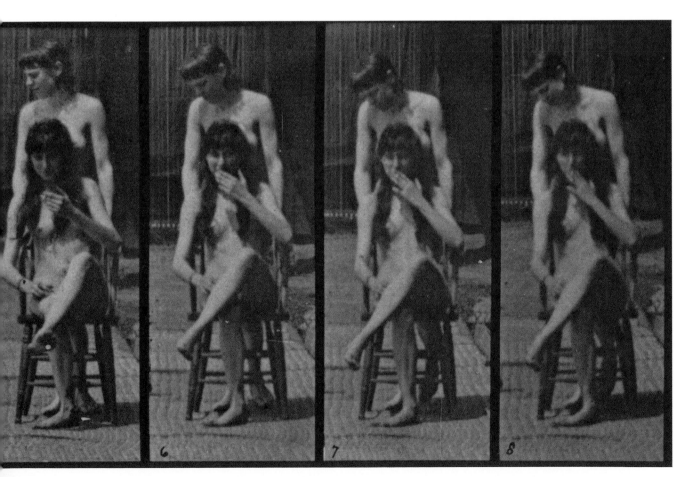

THE PASSION OF JOAN OF ARC

1928, CARL THEODOR ĐREYER

The Eyes Have It

It seems like a big jump from 1887 to 1928, and I deserve to be criticized for my indifference to and neglect of those decades in between. I will admit that I am omitting many great things (like Griffith's close-ups of Lillian Gish, or Eisenstein's cartoony head shots), and this book is so selective it may seem capricious. But I don't know that I would ever have fallen in love with silent cinema.

Still, one thing emerges in my chronological sequence (if you are reading the book in that obedient way): While Eadweard Muybridge was a very daring pioneer and an historical figure beyond dispute, his daring did not extend to the close-up. Nowadays, his love of the full figure is refreshing. It is a reminder, or a prediction, of the cinema of Renoir, Hawks, Mizoguchi, and Max Ophüls. But his fascination with human motion did not extend to the smile or the frown. Perhaps he didn't quite notice them.

So Carl Dreyer's *The Passion of Joan of Arc* suddenly insists on the close-up—the face—and there are other moments in this book (*Birth*, *Heat*, *The Shop Around the Corner*) that are celebrations of that kind of shot. I don't really mean to select one special close-up of Renée Falconetti's Joan, though I do want to stress the way Rudolph Maté filmed her in a flat morning light (using the new panchromatic film stock and no makeup, which made for a scathing, cleansing effect). Equally, anyone has to concede the intensity of the actress's openness to the camera and to the enquiry or process of the film. It can never be said that Falconetti did not know she was making a movie—in those days the camera would have had to be very close to her, and Dreyer was a director who talked to his players a great deal to build up the mood. (Such coaching was common in silent films. Actors by necessity became more alone, or inward, with sound.) Nor is Joan, in the twentieth century and at the height of the Jazz Age, the easiest role to bring alive. I admire Jean Seberg and Sandrine Bonnaire in later versions (by Otto Preminger and Jacques Rivette), but I don't think they were as capable of the

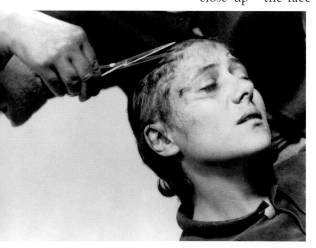

Renée Falconetti's Joan.

16

*Falconetti as
Jeanne d'Arc.*

commitment made by Falconetti, just as neither of the later directors was close to sharing Dreyer's own faith. Falconetti's only rival is the actress in Bresson's Joan of Arc film—whose name I have to look up: it is Florence Carrez in *The Trial of Joan of Arc.* Then there is Ingrid Bergman, not at her finest moment, and don't forget Hedy Lamarr's Joan in *The Story of Mankind* (1957).

The crucial insight with Dreyer's film is that there is just one close-up of Joan that lasts out the entire film, with cutaways to other faces or actions. It is as if we are looking at Joan so steadily that we become her or fall into her mind and anticipate her responses. By "passion" Dreyer meant a transcendent spiritual experience, the matter of approaching God and sublimity—if you like. But there is another passion that the age of movies liked much more, or more comfortably, which is that of being as one with a face on the screen. Yes, it is often fantasy and mere eroticism, so it can bring on great frustration. But it is an imaginative leap. So this kind of moment is reiterated throughout the history of cinema. It is just that no one has ever surpassed Dreyer and Falconetti—though Anna Karina watching the film in Godard's *Vivre Sa Vie* (1962) is a contender.

I hope this is not read as disrespect, but Joan may not be your type of young woman. She's not mine. Still, one may come closer to understanding religious experience by watching movies—especially those of Bresson—than from hours in church or reading religious literature or looking at paintings of Madonnas and crucifixions. I think that is because of the yearning for belief and transcendence that once existed in cinema. Once? you ask. I'm afraid so. Though I hope you will disagree.

And flesh in dread. Films of the spirit often have a hint of horror.

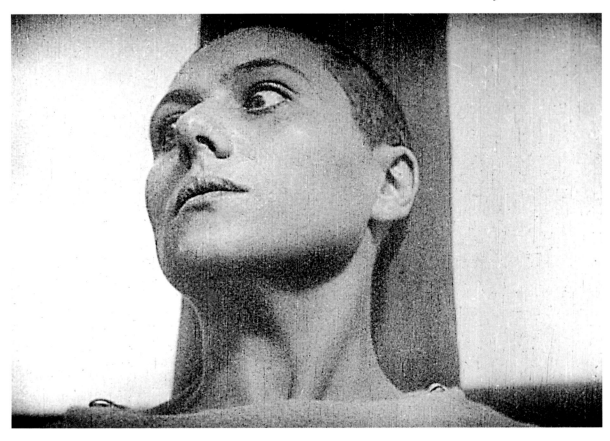

SUNRISE

1927, F. W. MURNAU

A Great Place of Fancy and Escape

We are on a grassy bank by a lake, or is it marshland? There is a sheen in the moonlight that is dreamy but dangerous. A huge, untidy man (George O'Brien) is lying on the ground in the arms of a dark-haired, chic woman dressed in black (Margaret Livingston). She is from the city and he is a farmer. She has come visiting—but why, unless it is to seduce him? And it has worked. He is stricken, or half asleep, quite taken over by her seductiveness. He is married (to the very sweet, blonde Janet Gaynor), with a child, but somehow this siren has won him over. We never know why, but his vulnerability seems a part of his discontent and his aptitude for violence.

It is a silent film, made by the German F. W. Murnau in America at the express and excited invitation of William Fox. The studio head told the world that this would be a great and artistic picture, deeper than most things attempted in America. Murnau had come with a German script and German designers, and he had set out to create a world that was half German folk tale and half Jazz-Age Manhattan. As she kisses and caresses the farmer, the dark woman tells him, "Come to the city." In 1927, the population-split between city and country in America was about equal, so this is a film that spoke to its moment, and to every married man who might think of another woman, one who might make love in a swamp and make you feel you were on the edge of a magical lake.

"And my wife?" he asks. He is an idiot, but he has a conscience. Where-upon the woman smiles at her own idea and suggests a faked boating accident. "Couldn't she get drowned?" she wonders. The titles are not printed, but written as if by hand. The word "drowned" comes in late and then that con-spiratorial sentence dissolves into the mist, like poison mingling with a clear solution.

The husband responds in shock and ferocity. He tries to strangle the city woman, but her sexuality and his desire overcome his righteousness, and then we get an extraordinary insight into the nature of the cinema. The illicit lovers sit up among the reeds, and then the lake and the sky, where the moon has been hanging like an eye, become a screen on which they watch a dazzling

"Come to the city."

"And my wife?"

OPPOSITE: *The City Woman and the Country Husband.*

21

"The scenes are not quite real but they are transporting . . ."

and enticing movie about the city itself—that great place of fancy and escape to which the woman is inviting him.

Murnau does that city as an advancing shot into a diorama, before tracking sideways rapidly over models, matte shots, dioramas, and God knows what—all of a sudden the as-yet unknown range of cinematic effects is poured out, like light or sex. The scenes are not quite real, but they are transporting and there is no doubt from the arrangement of the two figures that this is a commentary on the fantastical nature of film and the power of screens. The cityscape includes a jazz band and people dancing, and as we return to the bank in the country, so the city woman is doing her own slinky dance to the rhythm seen on the screen.

Of course, the entirety of *Sunrise* will show the farmer contrite and in love with his wife again after they

The city as a place of wonder and excitement where the couple are rescued.

have had a glorious day in the city—albeit a rather more sedate version of it than we have just encountered. *Sunrise* is often regarded as a great film. So be it; still, its very moral story arc is deeply at odds with the frenzied anticipation disclosed in this moment: That people look at a screened world and long to be there. It is a very American energy that tries to overcome destiny through sheer ambition or wanting.

That urge can murder if necessary—that's close to what happens in *A Place in the Sun* (1951), a film that could be played with *Sunrise* and in which Montgomery Clift goes to the chair eventually because, even though Shelley Winters died accidentally (in a boat on a dark lake), he had wanted her gone so that he could be with Elizabeth Taylor. And desire can murder reality.

OPPOSITE: *A swamp made in the studio.*

PANDORA'S BOX

1929, GEORG WILHELM PABST

Ecstatic, Dangerous, Impetuous and Reckless

BELOW AND OPPOSITE:

In Pandora's Box, *Lulu (Louise Brooks) intends to bring every man to her level. But is that going down or coming up?*

Recently, I heard the actress Geena Davis saying that to this day movies had far more male characters than female. Among extras, the disparity was even more pronounced. Yet the greatest unfairness of all persists in direction and running studios. For over a hundred years, the movies have done little to move away from the transaction of women being looked at by men, and smiling. But here is a picture and a moment where the woman gazes back with shocking insolence.

Louise Brooks was beautiful and very intelligent—not a combination the film business has ever been comfortable with. She did some American films (like *Beggars of Life* by William Wellman, and *A Girl in Every Port* by Howard Hawks). But when she asked Paramount for a raise, they said no way and told

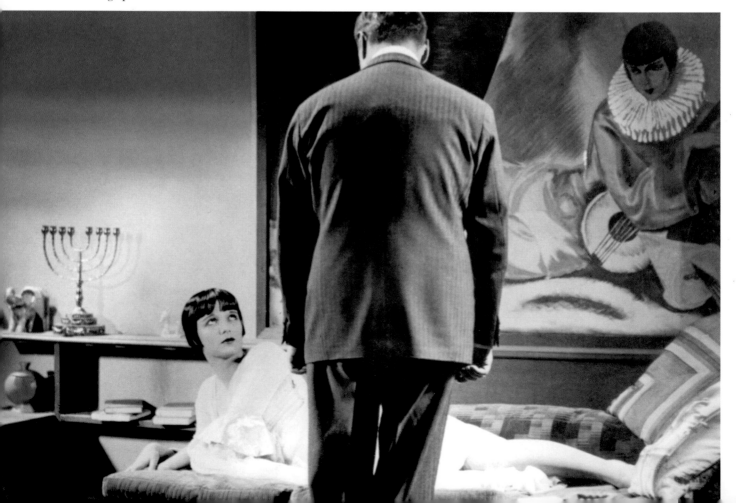

her instead that a German director, G. W. Pabst, had written asking if he could borrow her or have her for a movie adaptation of two plays by Frank Wedekind. They would be combined around the character of a beguiling whore, Lulu, who cut a swathe through society before Jack the Ripper killed her. On impulse, Brooks was interested and so she went to Berlin.

You could take nearly any shot of her from what is still a silent film. This is one of the most complete, ecstatic, impetuous and reckless performances anyone had ever given on screen. Indeed, it makes Marlene Dietrich in *The Blue Angel* seem coy and calculated. The thing about Brooks—and this is heaven at the end of moralistic and signposted silent cinema—is that no one knows what she's going to do next. I don't mean to say she was not under Pabst's control and design (though their bond was nowhere near as complete as that between Dietrich and Josef von Sternberg), but Brooks is a flame fluttering in the wind of her own breath. She is danger as it had not been seen or felt before.

The moment I choose is her complete enslavement of Dr. Schön (Fritz Kortner), the most authoritative man in the world around Lulu, wealthy, respected, solidly built, handsome in a brutal way. He is besotted with her and

he assumes that she is his for the taking—after all, what is she? So Lulu plays him like a fat, lazy fish and drags him down.

A show is being prepared and Lulu is supposed to play a part in it. But at the key moment, no one can find her. She is in a private room with Schön, and they are discovered by Schön's son, Alwa (Franz Lederer), another of Lulu's victims. The door opens and we see Schön collapsed like a drugged figure in Lulu's lap on the floor, apparently exhausted by lovemaking. At which point she looks up at Alwa, the camera and the world as if to say, "Well, what did you expect? He's crazy about me, and a girl likes to be obliging sometimes." Her dress is so relaxed it nearly reveals her breasts. Her smile is still modern and piercing, and you feel giddiness almost as if this Lulu could drag the world down. Yes, she is a femme fatale, to be sure. But you notice how far a femme fatale knows that her destructive path has doom as its only terminus.

It is a sensational film moment, and the still was admired in its day, but Brooks never

sustained a career. She came back to America after a few films in Europe and she let herself drift away from movies. She was a kept woman (with her own Schöns) and then a figure waiting in Rochester, New York, to be rediscovered. It happened. And today she is probably more famous than crowds of silent movie goddesses who far surpassed her in the twenties. Her influence is prodigious. Alban Berg began to write his opera *Lulu* in 1929, and it is the story that still occupies the stage and ballet companies. That haircut has become chic for decades and women seem to find insolence and defiance more natural and entertaining. If you try to imagine that Lulu meeting and having a conversation with Griffith's Lillian Gish, you may begin to appreciate how far the screen was changing behavior. Sometimes one film can do it. Or one scene.

Louise Brooks and Lulu gaze at us, one of the great knowing glances in cinema that recognizes the army of voyeurs in the dark.

27

MOROCCO

1930, JOSEF VON STERNBERG

The Orgy Commenced

I n his 1992 biography, *Marlene Dietrich: Life and Legend*, Steven Bach called it "the most memorable enunciation of sexual ambiguity in any picture." Amy Jolly was Dietrich's role in *Morocco*, the first picture she made in America after Josef von Sternberg had chosen her for *The Blue Angel*. The two of them were in love, or sex, or partnership—how are these things to be disentangled?—and the story goes that Dietrich herself found the novel on which the film was based. Then again, the film was based on no one but Marlene, and it was meant to tell America and Paramount what an emphatic if mysterious figure she was.

The scene is French North Africa (as reconstructed on a studio lot). Amy has come by boat to be an entertainer in a night club. The captain of the ship implies that she is a "suicide passenger"—she won't be going back. There must be something in her past; it is the condition of the Foreign Legion.

But this is her debut performance at the night club. In her dressing room she puts on a man's evening dress and tails and a top hat, and that appearance does not go down well with the crowd when she first appears. She is not put out or dismayed: Effrontery is her essence. But one member of

the audience, the legionnaire Tom Brown (Gary Cooper), is intrigued, and he silences the rowdy audience for her.

She sings "Quand l'Amour Meurt" with irony and panache, as if it might be a good thing to see that white elephant out of the way so that sweeter pursuits could be enjoyed. She plays games with the brim of her top hat, salutes that are as insolent as they are respectful. It is not just her prowess as a singer but her superb indifference that wins applause.

Then she notices a pretty dark-haired girl (Eve Southern) in the audience, and she looks at her with interest and amusement. The girl giggles, embarrassed by the scrutiny. Whereupon Amy goes up to the girl, lifts a flower from her hair and kisses her on the mouth. The girl dissolves, but not quite in shame, and Amy tosses the flower to Tom Brown who gives her a salute that she picks up on her way with the brim of her hat. He puts the flower behind his ear.

I suppose in hindsight it's a disappointment that, being courted by Tom Brown, Amy doesn't go home with the dark-haired girl—or both of them. But the suggestiveness made its mark. Dietrich's American career was established, and she and von Sternberg were off on a series of films that stand as a strange set of sadomasochistic home movies—though *home* is not the best word perhaps. Some in the audience may have just thought, Look at that nerve! But the way Amy surveys the girl is startlingly candid. It's like the way Gary Cooper looked at a woman in those days, and Cooper seems to get the point.

At the end of the film, Dietrich's Amy has become slave to a man, because of love. So she follows Brown's troop into the desert, unashamed to be with the Arab camp followers, the whores, and the riffraff. I think Dietrich herself was a more adroit survivor, just as in her personal life she was a pioneer figure in celebrated bisexuality—in other words, she was not bothered about keeping it secret. So the film or the studio tried to erase the implications of the night-club scene, but it's the moment that is anthologized and we see it now as one of the frankest and earliest admissions that watching the movies was the threshold to bisexuality. The orgy had commenced.

" . . . one of the . . . earliest admissions that watching the movies was the threshold to bisexuality."

" Dietrich was never really a great actress. "

Dietrich was never really a great actress. When asked to act she lost confidence. If told to exist she became a lighthouse summoning every sailor to her rocks. So truly the moment is weightier than the film and more enduring. But these days people like to take their films in bits and pieces—video allowed that—so one day it may be that no one makes full movies any longer, just arresting moments.

Is it Road to Morocco, *the finale of* Morocco *or an outtake from* The Sheltering Sky?

M

Irresistible Impulse

In the unnamed city, in the stage-bound city of German cinema, where the sun rarely shines, there has been a series of child killings. The parents are anxious. The police are doing all they can. Even the underworld is alarmed, because crimes like these can so easily disturb the orderly business of criminal activity. So the scum of the streets are on the lookout for suspicious people while the children themselves sing macabre songs in Fritz Lang's film:

"Just you wait a little while,
The evil man in black will come.
With his little chopper,
He will chop you up."

As it happens, the murderer himself looks like a plump, wide-eyed child. Peter Lorre was twenty-seven when *M* opened. His real name was Laszlo Lowenstein. He was a Hungarian Jew who had won an outstanding reputation in German theater for his daring and often surreal work. The story goes that Fritz Lang had seen him several years before *M*—in fact, before he had an idea of the film to come—and told him to be ready. It is one of the great performances in cinema history, but in an odd way it killed or restricted Lorre's career.

The film presents this killer as the helpless victim of irresistible impulse— the script was by Lang's wife of that period, Thea von Harbou. So a great deal of the film is composed, if not exactly from his point of view, while seeing him as the protagonist. We do not watch him kill a child (that is a kindness to us, perhaps, but it is a courtesy to his character, too; it makes him more acceptable). But we see him finding children, talking to them, and picking them up for murder. He comes upon a little girl, and they look at toys in a shop window.

Some of the street beggars are on to him, and one of them takes a piece of white chalk and inscribes a large *M* on the palm of his hand. Then he bumps into the killer, as if by accident, and prints an M on the back of his dark coat. This coat is as long as a shroud and it makes Lorre an expressive but inelegant figure.

"Uncle, you're all dirty."

OPPOSITE: *M is for murder and mirror, mirror on the street ... the killer (Peter Lorre) realizes that he has been identified.*

33

For several minutes, the murderer is unaware of the incriminating mark. But then the little girl sees it and she tells him, "Uncle, you're all dirty." He is mystified, until the great moment—it is a famous still in film history—when he thinks to look in a mirror and sees the *M*. It is a medium close-up of two figures: the face gazing at the glass, the glaring M on the coat, and the terrified face in the mirror, looking back at being noticed. Both heads wear rhyming fedora hats. Very few directors ever composed shots better than Lang, and in a way this brief vision is the whole film (the cameraman was Fritz Arno Wagner).

It is the end of the murderer's privacy. He knows he is identified and he must be sure that he will be caught. But the image has much deeper psychological meanings. This is the instant in which he comes face-to-face with his nature, and in fact it subtly undermines the script's proposition that he cannot help himself. There is a part of his soul that does observe himself. More than that, the mirror is a screen within the screen, and it begins to raise the question, Why is it in the movie dark we are so drawn to murderers when in life they are so dreadful? But no film before *M* had understood this.

Beyond that, Lorre was seeing his own future. *M* was a sensation, and it promoted the actor from German work to an international level. But, coupled with his very unusual looks, he was going to be forever typecast as a killer or a madman. It was really only as Mr. Moto, the grotesque stereotype Japanese detective, that he escaped that mark.

This grown up boy would hardly hurt a fly, would he? At 27, Lorre could still suggest a child.

Of course, Lorre is still known. He is in classics, like *The Maltese Falcon* and *Casablanca*, and he had a unique voice and presence. But it was hardly the career he might have hoped for. He was only fifty-nine when he died, a drug addict and a lost soul. Actors yearn to have a breakthrough role, but sometimes it breaks them, too.

The killer and the child in a crowded toy shop. Yet again, this image relies on glass, and our looking through the window.

20,000 YEARS IN SING SING

1933, MICHAEL CURTIZ

Now Voyeur

Tommy Connors (Spencer Tracy) is a man-about-town gangster shipped up to Sing Sing on a five-to-thirty-year sentence. He thinks his crooked lawyer (Louis Calhern) will finesse his release fast, so he acts cocky. But the warden (based on the reformer, Warden Lewis Lawes) gets him to shape up to prison life. He's beginning to face reality by the time his girlfriend, Fay (Bette Davis), comes to visit him.

The gowns credit on the picture goes to Orry-Kelly, an Australian (real name John Kelly) who had wanted to act but gave that up for clothes. Fay comes calling in one of the great dresses in film history, and it's an intriguing fact that women looked at their best in movies in the depth of the Depression. It's a calf-length dress, flared from just above the knee, a flamboyant and unrepentant celebration of deco black and white, with white side panels, a white fur stole, a black bow at the neck and a fallen breast line. Fay wears a flat white ribbon and a scoop of black hat in her platinum blond hair. The only dark in her face comes in her eyes, and her false lashes.

I suppose it's a matter of conventional wisdom that Davis was not as beautiful as many stars of her time, but whenever I see her in the early thirties, I doubt the sense in that verdict. She is a knockout, all the more so because she is smarter than her rivals. Tracy obviously thinks so. He is so aroused by her great look and the slender way she fills the dress that he is disturbed. She dolled up for Tommy; she wanted to look her best for him. But her success is driving him wild. The visiting area is not private, and there are black iron railings that keep them apart, though there is kissing and touching (he rests his head on her arm). When Tracy utters the rather plain line, "I'd give a million bucks to be alone with you for a little while," we believe him, we have one more chance to see how Tracy could make the commonplace authentic, and we do not question the chemistry they had together.

The barrier to sex, here in 1933 (a key moment in the onset of the Hays Code), is more erotic than any actual love scene of that era—or much later. Tracy and Davis were not raised to make love, or pretend to do it, on screen. But they knew how to look at each other with longing and desire. One profound reason for that is that they can get very little closer to each other

> " . . . women looked at their best in movies in the depth of the Depression."

OPPOSITE: *Are you looking at me or the dress—or the way the two go together?*

37

than we can come to them. On-screen desire is a replica of our yearning in the dark. So our eyes become sexual organs and voyeurism is launched.

Here's the ultimate sadness. This is the only picture Tracy and Davis would ever make together. No matter that their careers were just getting started (he was eight years older than Bette). He had been loaned from Fox to First National (a department of Warner Bros., Bette's studio and ordeal until the mid-1940s). Anyone could see they were made for each other in 1933, and Tracy was not often sexy on screen, or not in a direct way—was he a little shy? By 1935 Tracy was taken up by MGM, and that's where he did his famous films, and met Katharine Hepburn.

Now, no one wants to live without Spence & Kate, but did they have the kind of physical bond that makes Tracy nearly growl in *20,000 Years*? Suppose Tracy had stayed at Warner Bros., imagine what he and Bette might have done together . . . or did Davis need weaker or more passive men as she grew stronger? Still, Tracy might have been Rick in *Casablanca* (we know he responded to Ingrid Bergman—and Michael Curtiz directed this film and *Casablanca*). And so a moment can turn into a lifetime of speculation.

Their only time on screen together:
Bette Davis and Spencer Tracy.

DODSWORTH

1936, WILLIAM WYLER

Toward Literature

There are piercing instants that need preamble. In William Wyler's *Dodsworth* (1936), Sam Dodsworth (Walter Huston), an automobile tycoon from "Zenith" in Sinclair Lewis's 1929 novel on Midwest success, has sold his company and elected to take his wife, Fran (Ruth Chatterton), to Europe. Sam isn't quite sure what he wants out of Paris, but Fran wants adventure. She flirts with attractive men and denies her real age (forty-one). Sam sees the sights and Fran collects possible escorts. There is a dinner party in the Dodsworths' hotel suite for eight people, including Arnold Iselin (Paul Lukas) and Edith Cortright (Mary Astor), a woman the Dodsworths met on the boat to France.

It looks like a stage, but Wyler's camera brings it to life.

As the evening breaks up, Fran declares that it was in celebration of her birthday—she is . . . thirty-five. Ruth Chatterton was forty-four. There is a cut to a wry smile on Sam's face—Sam is plain, decent, honest, vigorous, an authentic American entrepreneur, but he loves Fran and abides by her fibs.

Edith Cortright says she had no idea it was Fran's birthday—Mary Astor was thirty, and at her peak. Wyler covers their following talk in conventional two-shots and close-ups, but if the lines are good and the players alert, the cinema has no richer vein.

Mrs. Cortright says, "When you're my age, you will look back on thirty-five as a most agreeable time of life."

Fran senses danger, but she defies the flagrant evidence of the camera: "I hope I look as young as you do when I'm your age."

To which Edith replies, "You're almost sure to, my dear."

Fran: the desire and the uncertainty.

Seventy-five years later, the viewer has to urge himself to keep up with the wit and innuendo of these lines, but the guide is the kindly pity on Edith Cortright's face, which has let us feel the lie and the foolish vanity that will destroy the Dodsworth marriage. So what we are asked to recognize is not just simple human observation, but a kind of moral judgment, too. In a story (it might not happen in life), Edith and Sam are made for each other, even though Edith has tried to rescue her rival. And it happens in seconds.

At this point, Mrs. Cortright goes away to find her coat. Sam takes other guests to the elevator and Fran is left alone with Lukas as Iselin. In murmured words, their relationship deepens, but Edith returns to notice this. Not that Wyler is vulgar enough to give us her shocked reaction in close-up.

Instead, we get this instant of intense beauty. Mrs. Cortright comes close to Fran. We have a superb close-up of Astor. She tells Fran, very softly, with sadness and hope, "My dear—don't."

"What?" says Fran, in a cross-cut close-up. She is startled and stupid, too. She has been placed.

And then Astor's gaze just drifts sideways to rest on Iselin. She does not mention his name or spell anything out. We have no need of that. And if we see the film more than once, we may even perceive how far Edith has already seen ahead and wondered what it all might mean for her.

This is just nine years after the labored and often telegraphed discourse of silent film. The cameraman here is Rudolph Maté, who had photographed the agonized and exhilarated expressions on the face of Falconetti in *The Passion of Joan of Arc*. But by 1936 we had the opportunity for a few words and the kind of underplaying they allow. The vault in sophistication is breathtaking.

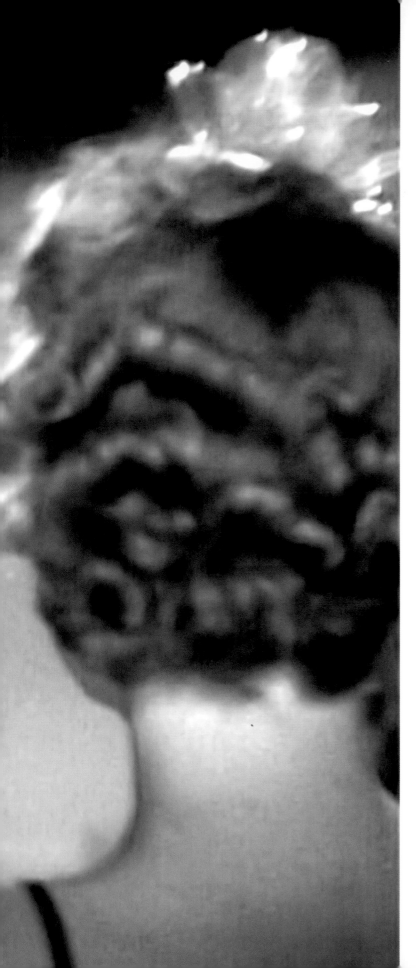

"My dear—don't."

Sidney Howard wrote the lines, Wyler has shot them, and Huston, Astor, Lukas and Chatterton have lifted us to the level of reality and subtext that exists in the moment from Henry James's *Portrait of a Lady* where Isabel Archer sees Osmond and Madame Merle standing together and understands their history and her defeat.

Dodsworth becomes a graver film in this scene. One love story starts as another ends. And it is prompted by the face of Mary Astor, whose own reckless diaries (on her sexy affair with George S. Kaufman) were even then being bandied about in a divorce action taken by her outraged husband. Astor was only thirty, but she seems so experienced. Life shows in the face. This is what movie could do once it had sound: It veered away from theater and moved toward literature.

Getting to know each other:
Walter Huston and Mary Astor.

BRINGING UP BABY

1938, HOWARD HAWKS

Sexual Riot

Their first meeting is disastrous in ways that can never be forgotten—no matter how long they stay together. David Huxley (Cary Grant) is a leading paleontologist whose life's quest is the assembling of a complete brontosaurus skeleton—though he lacks the intercostal clavicle. Almost without noticing, David has become engaged to an unsuitable and unpleasant woman. He is also trying to raise more money for his bone project. One day, he meets Susan Vance (Katharine Hepburn) who seems to be moderately wealthy, a good golfer, chronically impulsive or wild in her ways and with little else to do except threaten his sanity and fog his spectacles. Of course, he will admit later how in the quiet moments he might begin to find her attractive; it's just that there aren't any quiet moments.

They run into each other at a country club where David arrives in tails and a top hat, in search of funds. Susan employs accident as a love signal, and so she rips the back of his tails, and then in short order the back of her dress is torn, too, revealing her panties. With difficulty, he signals this mishap to her and suddenly her assurance is wiped away so that David is compelled to stand behind her, cover her panties with his battered top hat and frog-march her away to safety, or a dressing room.

You can guess that *Bringing Up Baby* was attempting to be a comedy, though it did not fare well at the box office. It was written by Dudley Nichols and Hagar Wilde and directed by Howard Hawks, and I have little hesitation now in acclaiming it as a screwball masterpiece. But it is a picture that alerts us to the endless favorite sport in Hawks—he was obsessed with sex as a screen topic—you did hear that in life he was very limited in its application. This seems to me central, for Hawks was a fantasist, far more comfortable imagining than doing. As a result, the grand ideals themselves—love and adventure—are always subject to mockery in Hawks, or an unforgiving disbelief. It is what keeps him so modern.

So here we are in 1938 with a top hat firmly applied to a young woman's bottom and her silky underwear, and we are meant to be howling with laughter. But if Luis Buñuel, say—not that Buñuel was making films in 1938—had tried it, the scene would almost certainly have been banned. Comedy seldom

"It is a moment of glory."

Are you looking at me or the dress?

Are you following me?

Oh, you've torn your coat!

received Oscars, but it could get away with murder. It's enough to make you wonder where the word *screwball* came from and to note that it might be thought to have powerful sexual connotations.

So the mastery of *Bringing Up Baby* alludes to more than Hawks, Grant and Hepburn (a trio capable of as much intelligent mischief as the Marx Brothers). It is a way of saying that screwball, and even gentler forms of comedy, were the most daring genres Hollywood ever permitted itself. By the end of this film, David has his bone in place—in every sense you can imagine. He has forsaken his fiancée and he is with Susan, willing to announce—from his academic height—that the farce and disorder of their recent lives have been

Oh, look what's happened to your hat!

fun. No one pauses to define fun, or think of showing its destiny, and both Grant and Hepburn were fairly reserved romantically on screen. But the hat and the underpants give the game away. This is a film about sexual riot (with a tactful unacademic slant), in which cross talk and slapstick do everything that naked bodies were not allowed to do. It is a moment of glory, and soon enough Hollywood decided that it was out of the past and ought not to be encouraged. So naked bodies and dirty language came in in the sixties and fun was not seen for decades. It may still be hiding somewhere in the deep woods of Connecticut.

GONE WITH THE WIND

1939, VICTOR FLEMING

A Frequent Sense of the Momentous

At not much short of four hours, *Gone With the Wind* has plenty of moments, and a frequent sense of the momentous: You could pick the open-air casualty station on the streets of Atlanta, with the crane shot culminating in the tattered flag; you could have the collected conversations between

Rhett and Scarlett, building to the way he carries her up the grand staircase; you could have the ending of the first part, with the agonized tree in silhouette against a bloodstained sunset; you could choose him leaving without a damn, and her determining that she'll think about that tomorrow, or another day.

It's a spectacular melodrama, a key achievement in Technicolor and a celebration of design, including the work of designer William Cameron Menzies, costumier Walter Plunkett and Jack Cosgrove, who did so many exquisite painted glasses to stand in for the backgrounds of the South. Indelibly, it has Vivien Leigh, and the intense sympathy between her Scarlett and the film's producer, begetter and besetting problem, David O. Selznick. But if it is the all-time greatest box-office coup and the most famous film, I'm not sure if it has scenes that quite live up to its grand reputation.

The wounded at Atlanta. One observer said, "If we'd had that many troops, the South would have won the war."

"It was as if we had never seen a film before."

The key to *Gone With the Wind* is the impact it had in theaters, the very occasion of it. So I am choosing two special performances of the film.

The first was a painfully hot Saturday evening in September 1939 when a line of cars drove out to Riverside, California, to stage an impromptu preview—a sneak. It involved Selznick and his wife Irene, their partner Jock Whitney, the film's editor James Newcomb, and carloads of cans of film in double-system, the picture and the sound separate. They came to a theater and Newcomb and Selznick went in to speak to the manager. He had a pretty full house and he was showing *Hawaiian Nights* and *Beau Geste*. They asked if they could slip their picture in between the two features—and that night their cut must have been well over four hours. Selznick told the manager who he was and by the number of cans the fellow guessed what the picture was.

So it was all set up and when the title came on, the audience went mad—this was only the most publicized film of all time, and they had that special feeling that roasting night of being so lucky to see it first. It was immediately clear that, whatever the doubters said—and they existed—this picture was going to be an exceptional event, maybe the picture of pictures.

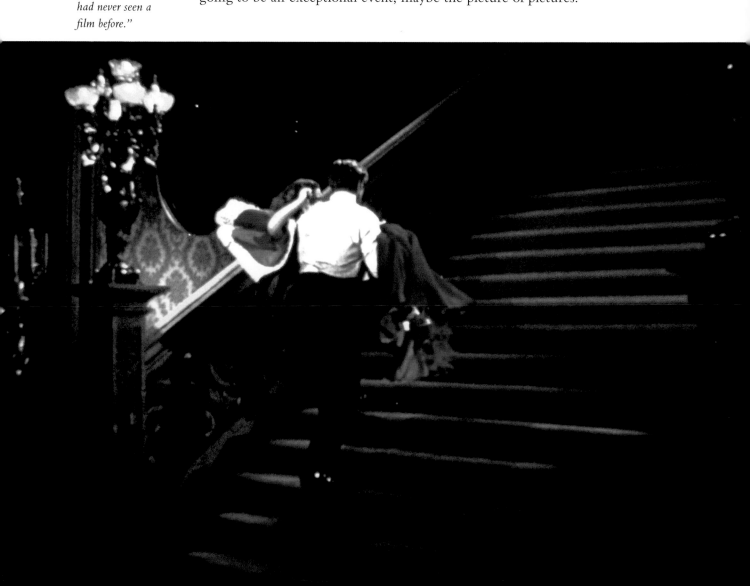

But Hollywood would never have the innocence of 1939 again. As the movie opened, Europe was at war and the first viewers of the film were hit by the meaning of war's damage.

The second screening was December 15, 1939, the world premiere of the picture with so many people in attendance: Vivien Leigh and Laurence Olivier, Clark Gable and Carole Lombard, Olivia de Havilland, the book's author Margaret Mitchell and Evelyn Keyes, who played one of Scarlett's sisters. She recalled it this way: "When the interval came, there was absolute silence in the theater. It was as if we had never seen a film before."

At the end of the second half, there were torrents of applause. The film began to take more money—counting dollars at their worth at the point of purchase—than any other film has ever done. The celebration was immense and it culminated in the Oscars. But not everyone went to Atlanta for the opening. Selznick had put Hattie McDaniel (Mammy) on the list of guests, but the people in Atlanta said they hoped there could be a change of mind on that matter to avoid local embarrassment. Selznick was outraged. He protested. But the actress did not make the journey. Of course, in time she won the Oscar for best supporting actress—the first Oscar to a black player. You might have imagined that Selznick would have had her at the large central table for the *Wind* people. Not so. At the Academy Award ceremony, Hattie McDaniel and her companion were at a small table for two, off in a corner of the big room. Moments.

"At the Academy Award ceremony, Hattie McDaniel and her companion were at a small table for two, off in a corner of the big room."

THE SHOP AROUND THE CORNER

1940, ERNST LUBITSCH

The Absence of a Letter

In the comedy of conversation and behavior, there are likely to be fewer set-piece moments such as may easily be put on display. In no other genre is the quality of the picture so dependent on flow and consequence. And so it is that production stills from our best talking comedies tend to be two-shots or groups. The people are interesting but you know it's the talk that matters. When people spoke of the Lubitsch "touch" they wanted to suggest the presence of ironic grace notes that were vital to Ernst Lubitsch's way of looking at the world, and they often turned on the small, undignified gap between pose and practice, truth and lies. But on screen, the famous touch was frequently the way in which the film had someone say something that was revealing or absurd. And deeply human. The old convention of stills doesn't help Lubitsch too much because his movies were about someone saying something odd, or off, and someone else giving a wry look—at the world of reason or the possibility of an audience there, watching.

So on the one hand, *The Shop Around the Corner* is as frivolous as building a pretty, Christmas-season Budapest on the MGM sound stages when the real Budapest had so much to worry about (you can turn to those worries in the remarkable *To Be Or Not To Be* [1942]), but for the moment, in 1940, all Lubitsch is worried about is whether Alfred (James Stewart) and Klara (Margaret Sullavan) can muster the good sense to realize that they are made for each other.

Look at all they have in common: They work at Matuschek's, the best gift shop in the city; they are honest and decent, but they are both just a little too proud or priggish and fatally inclined to look for more respectable bonds of affection than being attracted; and they are the stars of our show so we know where they are headed in the Arden of Matuschek's—if they have the sense to admit love and need.

Another thing they have in common is that they are both engaged in writing love letters to someone they have never met. Each other. But the obstacle to that is that they both earnestly believe that they do not like the other person, the real writer, very much.

"She was as good as we ever had."

53

" If this
woman
cannot
absorb
the truth,
she might
go mad."

As in many great tiny stories, the intrigue becomes very complicated. You have to see it and follow the cunning delicacy of Samson Raphaelson's script as well as Lubitsch's discreet way of noticing detail. But a moment comes when Klara desperately requires a letter from her pen pal, and it is not going to be there. This is what Lubitsch does. His camera is in an impossible position—but who cares? It is behind the wall of mailboxes at a post office. To be precise, it is behind Klara's box. All that happens is that she comes to open her box and it lets us see her searching eyes and mounting dismay as she sees the empty box. This inner frame concentrates on her and it permits a hint of prison, or even tragedy. Moreover, it is just the way of looking at Margaret Sullavan that may entertain the realization that she was more than just a pretty, smart face and a hushed, romantic voice. She was romantic tragedy. She was as good as we ever had. And suddenly we notice that the game and the whimsy of *The Shop Around the Corner* are close to very dangerous ground. If this woman cannot absorb the truth, she might go mad.

Klara is waiting for "him," but Alfred realizes who "she" is.

James Stewart and Margaret Sullavan were fond friends; there may have been a time when they were more than that. In their several films together, there is a lovely feeling of attentiveness and caring between them. And there was also the odd way in which sometimes his voice seemed higher than hers. This is their masterpiece, just as it is one of our great comedies. Sullavan was married a lot—to William Wyler, Henry Fonda and Leland Hayward—and she had a hard time being bounced from happiness to unhappiness. She went deaf, too early, she was depressed, and she killed herself at the age of fifty. Is it fanciful to predict that simply from her agonized face in the mailbox?

Margaret Sullavan and James Stewart—one of the great pairings in movie romance.

55

THE LETTER

In the Beginning

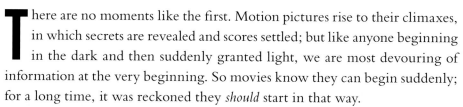

"There are no moments like the first."

There are no moments like the first. Motion pictures rise to their climaxes, in which secrets are revealed and scores settled; but like anyone beginning in the dark and then suddenly granted light, we are most devouring of information at the very beginning. So movies know they can begin suddenly; for a long time, it was reckoned they *should* start in that way.

So it's fascinating with *The Letter* to see how far the apparatus or logo of the film, its credit sequence, its business credentials, facilitate the opening of the story. That works in three main ways: First, the credits are as quick as they decently can be, and they play over scenes of the Malaya where the action takes place; second, the music is in the same atmospheric key—indeed, the music that introduced Warner Bros. films in 1940 (stirring, arousing, but full of threat or danger, too) was by the Max Steiner who did the score that runs through *The Letter*; and third, there is a luster in the black and white of the Warner Bros. shield logo and the credit sequence that is attuned to the day-for-night texture of the establishing scenes behind the credits. As far as possible, therefore, going to the movies, being there in the dark, has been put in rhythm and sync with the first frames of film and the first moment of story.

Not that the credits go so swiftly as to be beyond discussion. The Warner logo, which seems set in old stone (after all, the studio had been in action nearly twenty years by then!), merges into a handwritten font for the titles— why not when the film is called *The Letter*, in a time and place when that meant handwriting. Then notice the solo credit for Bette Davis; the shared credit for Somerset Maugham (whose play *The Letter* comes from) and William Wyler, the film's director; and the smaller type against the title that admits that Jack L. Warner was "In Charge of Production."

No one in 1940 was expected to agonize over authorship of a movie. For the public, the emphatic presence of Bette Davis was everything, and Maugham and Wyler were as much in her service as wardrobe and makeup. But the mock-modest insistence on Jack Warner is not simply the ego of the tycoon, it is the reminder to the world and to Bette Davis of ownership. Only a few years before *The Letter*, Bette had tried to escape a contract with Warner Bros.—because, she

Bette Davis

in

"The Letter"

Jack L. Warner
In Charge of Production

complained, they were giving her lousy parts. She fled to England and Warners fought her in the London courts. Like a naughty girl she was told off, and ordered to honor her contract. Yet Warners did wake up, and *The Letter* is one of the much better parts that came her way thereafter (along with directors as thorough and tender as Wyler—he and Bette had an affair).

The music has altered as the story comes in, though not the instrumentation or the essential tone of warning and passion—we are talking here of something that everyone now recognizes and patronizes as "movie music." Yet it is better termed the oil of melodrama that sustains the exaggerated acting, the abrupt narrative, and the moodiness of the image. In short, the atmospheric of the film does not really build; it is close to hysteria from the outset. It has to be, for Leslie Crosbie's most naked feeling in the picture is here, right at the start.

I said the photography was day-for-night so that, with the use of the dark filter over the camera lens, an effect of night has been obtained while shooting in daylight. That was an economy that helped the film factory function in regular hours. But it also meant that night was visible, shaped by light, hot, and that bit more passionate or melodramatic. Real night is colder than day; it is so dark we cannot find our way, and we may be so tired we aren't as alert as we should be. Note how the opposite is true of this classic movie night.

We are in Malaya, the Malaya of Burbank, where the Warner studio was. The floor is smooth so that a camera can track over it. The sound stage is large enough for elaborate lighting schemes to pass as moonlight. And the foliage is décor—it may employ real botany, but plants chosen, shaped, polished, placed, and lit by art direction.

A sign tells us we are on a rubber plantation. There is a brief cutaway, with dripping music, to a rubber tree and the milky juice being extracted and collected in cups. This may be as much as some of us have ever learned about real rubber, but it is also helplessly sexual. No censor in 1940 needed to think the milky stuff was semen, but no audience member had to reject that thought, either. And if we have learned anything from movies it is how much of the undertone audiences get very fast.

The camera then tracks and cranes with great elegance over the rough accommodations of the natives on the plantation. They are resting or asleep. Some are playing games; others are supine in artfully lit hammocks. The attitude to Malaysians is not malicious or cruel, but it is effortlessly superior, and to that extent we are being set up for a jolt, for Maugham knew and Leslie Crosbie will learn that the obedient people who sustained this rubber empire had a grasp on irony, too.

As the camera continues this line of movement from left to right a shot is heard, and it disturbs a white cockatoo into flight. The bird has been aroused by something in the far distance: On the veranda of a large house, we see a

"We are in Malaya, the Malaya of Burbank..."

man emerge and then stagger, as if shot—why not, a gun has gone off. Notice that we never see this man's face, no matter that he has been Leslie Crosbie's lover, no matter if, finally, she can set the whole shame or disgrace of murder aside as being less than the way she misses this man. He preferred his native mistress, played by Gale Sondergaard, the film's supreme force of vengeance, whose masked look could be a model for Davis.

We cut in to a medium shot of the veranda steps and as we see or feel the man dropping out of sight, so the camera fixes on the figure of Leslie, advancing with implacable purpose, so as to be close enough to this man to keep hitting him with bullets. She wears a long dark dressing gown with flowing sleeves. She is composed, but fluent, as if liberated. And the camera adores her, looking up at her fierce compassionless face as she fires all six shots. The revolver clicks again—she would have kept firing forever perhaps. Then she lets the gun fall from her hand, the way Michael Corleone will be taught thirty-two years later. But her arm stays pointing and the camera closes in toward a medium shot on the indicated diagonal of her arm.

That is when we get Bette Davis—resplendent yet eroded, as ravaged as she is attractive, as tragic as she is nasty, her small pinched face quivering with tormented need. Bette Davis was a remarkable star, a very daring one, in that she hardly ever wasted time trying to be beautiful. Yet for decades, on-screen, she was an emblem of thwarted passion—she played romantically demanding women or tyrants, and it shows here. So we know straightaway, and we know it in that the man remains faceless, that her soon-to-be instruction to the servants that an "accident" has occurred, is not to be believed. We know already that this is not the kind of movie in which accident can ever stand up to destiny. Leslie Crosbie is dangerous and selfish, and she would have been the same in South Kensington as she is outside Singapore.

CITIZEN KANE

1941, ORSON WELLES

Mother and Child

Thompson (William Alland), the faceless reporter, has been admitted to the Thatcher Library, where every turned page echoes, and the light is from Valhalla, and the sacred manuscript of the Thatcher diary is brought before him. (Some things are treasured in America, but Kane's properties will be burnt in a furnace.)

As the camera sinks toward the diary, the white of the page turns into the white of snow on the voice-over: "I first encountered Mr. Kane in 1871 . . ." We are in a kind of Western, a cabin in the wilderness of Colorado, Mrs. Kane's Boarding House, and the banker Thatcher (George Coulouris) has come to take delivery of the boy, Charles Foster Kane.

The kid is outside in a cap and a muffler, playing, throwing snowballs. We see him through the square of a window from inside the cabin and we hear him shouting, "The Union forever." But the family he belongs to is being broken up. For fifty thousand dollars a year (it is spelled out) paid to Mr. and Mrs. Kane, the bank will take over and run the Colorado Lode mine (passed on to Mrs. Kane, regarded as worthless, in hopeless payment of a debt), and the boy will be taken East where "The Bank's decision in all matters concerning his education, his places of residence, and similar subjects, will be final."

OPPOSITE: *Citizen Kane, the cabin on the prairie— a lost home. The boy outside shouts, "The Union forever!" while his family is legally dissolved.*

"She sold him for $50,000 a year."

They are selling their son to the banker, and it is clear that the mother is decisive in this blunt action: "I've got his trunk all packed. I've had it packed for a week now." Surely a less firm mother or a more emotional woman would have put off that evil day.

What happens inside the cabin is the focus of our attention. The father (Harry Shannon) is feeble. He seems older than his wife (Agnes Moorehead). He hovers in the background. Her bold movements dominate the tracking camera. He closes a window but then immediately she throws it open. We see her in a medium shot, looking out, the cold light scathing her face. She cries "Charles!" and we hear the wind and the music at this brink of a moment. It is a terrible action of the mother's doing, yet she seems brimming with repressed regret. Is she truly sorry, or does the emotional energy come from Kane the dying man, decades later, trying to persuade himself the trade broke her heart? Because if it wasn't that devastating to her, then it destroyed his heart. And the possibility exists that *Citizen Kane*—despite all its novelty and cleverness, and its unprecedented use of "cinema"—is a tragedy about a man who lost everything that mattered. It is an American lesson that one thing you never get means more than all the things you obtain and amass.

Here, in the 21st century, we watch the 1941 evocation of the 1870s. Not the least power of film is to make us uncertain of time.

She sold him for $50,000 a year and the idea that the bank would look after him properly: It is the eternal struggle between independence and being governed, and that's why it's a scene from a Western.

The characters come out into the cold open air. This is not Colorado, and there is no sunlight. It is a set with fake snow and an overcast diorama with light that might have been imported from Germany (the photography is by Gregg Toland). Now we see the boy (Buddy Swan)—handsome, belligerent, vulnerable— and we witness the moment of his being handed over. He fights. He uses his plain wooden sled as a weapon. There is an endlessly ambiguous shot—a pan down from the mother's face to the boy's in an embrace—that is like a Madonna and child (her name is Mary), or the witch clutching Hansel.

Then there are just dissolves on the sled left in the snow, with the pile of snow gathering on it like an overture to passing time. Welles once said that sled was only "dollar-book Freud," but some of Freud's messages were important and as instructive as the movies. Why shouldn't anyone with a dollar to spare have access to those things? When do we see *Citizen Kane* enough to realize that this famous young show-off, this precocious master of the new medium, made a great tragedy that quite reasonably had the working title of *American*?

OPPOSITE: *At the close of* Kane, *for just a few seconds we get an answer to "Rosebud." But then we have to wonder what answers mean.*

THE LADY EVE

1941, PRESTON STURGES

The Other War

"A man should have a hobby."

After a year up the Amazon, Pike (Henry Fonda) meets a new, adorable snake (Barbara Stanwyck).

Jean Harrington (Barbara Stanwyck) and her father, the "Colonel" (Charles Coburn), work cruise ships as cardsharps. Lo and behold, their liner pauses to pick up Charles Pike (Henry Fonda), the heir to a great beer fortune, who has just emerged from being up the Amazon studying snakes for a year. A man should have a hobby. Pike is stiff and stuffy, with very few attributes shared by the snakes he attends to, but Jean is a specimen. In the ship's dining room one night, while Charles is becoming increasingly flustered by the steady gaze of so many females interested in marrying into beer, Jean studies him in her compact mirror and assesses him as a chump. As he beats a retreat, he passes the Harringtons' table and Jean's slender sandaled foot is enough to trip him and send him flying.

Not that he is permitted to be the victim. No, he may have broken the heel on her shoe. The "pain" is such that he is obliged to help her back to her cabin, and there she goes to work on him. What follows is a sustained scene of conversation, seduction, and rising agitation and perplexity on Charles' part—though she gets around to calling him "Hoppsy." This is written and directed by Preston Sturges, and it is one of the great comedies in which Jean—having watched her father fleece Hoppsy at the card table—will be rejected by the Pike establishment, only to return masquerading as the "Lady Eve."

But let's linger in Jean's cabin along with Sturges's amused lubricity. There was a little history. Fonda and Stanwyck had just made *The Mad Miss Manton* together, and on that film Fonda had been haughty and condescending, failing to see that he was head-to-head with a brilliant comedienne and a very attractive woman. So one way or the other Sturges provided, and Stanwyck relished, a very sexy scene in which Pike hardly knows what is happening to him. He tries to be upright, but Jean is serpentine in her shapes and movement, and very solicitous of the numbing effect on an upright fellow with all that dry past up the Amazon. Later on, seeing how far her restless skirt has risen on her thigh (this was 1941) he makes a nervous adjustment to its hem, and Jean, drily, says, "Oh, thank you." That

64

may not read hilarious, but on-screen it is a moment to induce bliss, all the more intriguing because you can see how the much more sophisticated woman is beginning to fall for her target, the chump.

Nothing happens (this was 1941) in a modern sense, nothing beyond her mussing his hair and making sure that he's so close to her he can pick up her fragrance (not of the jungle) and notice things in nature he may not have seen before. Censorship, you see, or the accepted restraint of that time, had encouraged ways of being so suggestive that I swear audience temperatures rise in the course of the prolonged scene, with its complicated proximities. Sturges was not often a camera stylist, or a self-conscious filmmaker, but he lets this scene run several minutes and there is a stealthy build-up of sexual tension, no matter that Jean and Stanwyck are playing with Pike and enjoying their power. It's a touch cruel, but that was 1941.

This is relatively early in the film. There is far more to come, including Eugene Pallette as Pike's father and William Demarest as the family thug who insists it's "positively the same dame." I would urge you to see it and give yourself a real treat. Yet, on the other hand, I suspect you are younger than I am and not inclined to regard that as a handicap. So it's possible that you'd miss a lot of the charm, warmth and subtlety. I don't want to offend you in saying that, but 1941 was a good year in which the war between the sexes threatened to be as interesting and influential as the other war.

"...the woman is beginning to fall for her target, the chump."

CASABLANCA

1942, MICHAEL CURTIZ

Ready to Be a Sucker Again

As Time Goes By," was written, words and music, by Herman Hupfeld and it figured in a show, *Everybody's Welcome*, that played on Broadway in 1931. But not many people remembered it, despite a recording by Rudy Vallee. Nowadays, it is one of the most famous songs in all the movies, and with its refrain, "You must remember this, / A kiss is still a kiss," it represents a veil of nostalgia through which "old movies" are seen.

It had its second and essential life when a play, *Everybody Comes to Rick's*, was resuscitated, put through many hands and turned into the movie *Casablanca*. Folklore rejoices in all the traps and dead ends that the picture just survived (the other castings that were thought about, for example), but like most films of 1943—good or bad, or in between—it now looks and feels as if it was made by divine decision. Michael Curtiz, its director, had that knack: His best works looked no more decisive and emphatic than the bad pictures. Curtiz is still not regarded as a real auteur, despite *Casablanca*, *Yankee Doodle Dandy* (1942), and *Mildred Pierce* (1945). *Young Man with a Horn* (1950), a very entertaining but awful movie, has just the same confidence and élan.

In this case, I am being very obvious with my moment. I choose the scene, early on at the café, where Ilsa (Ingrid Bergman) and Victor (Paul Henreid) arrive and Ilsa approaches Sam (Dooley Wilson), the piano player. She asks him to play "As Time Goes By." Sam is reluctant. He can guess what's going to happen with that song out of the past. But he knows an irresistible script when it's given to him, no matter who really wrote this scene, so he starts the song and Rick, back in his office, hears it. How long has he been waiting to hear it? How much anger and recrimination is waiting for those few notes? Sure enough he comes striding onto the café floor, and he looks as mean and ugly as Bogart could manage, until he sees what there is to see and realizes what Sam is doing.

It's as corny as can be, yet like most movie clichés it's based on a universal knot of human behavior: re-encountering someone you loved once and realizing that the effort of forgetting, condemning

OPPOSITE AND BELOW:
*Sam's playing
my song.*

and turning bitter has had very little effect. You're ready to be a sucker again. But are you falling in love with the person or are you falling for the past, your own passage in time, and the mere idea of love? When you look at an old movie do you really re-examine it—do you look anew?—or are you falling in line with a version of yourself and your pleasure?

History says that *Casablanca* was a turning point in the war, in part because its invocation of a city not too many people could place was assisted by newspaper maps as the Allied efforts retook the real city. Then again, as Rick comes over from his cynical neutrality to join the war effort, the picture was said to have raised America's morale for the war. That's how it won Best Picture.

That all sounds like publicity. The atmosphere is terrific and the supporting cast (Greenstreet, Lorre, Veidt, Dalio, Claude Rains) is tiptop. But is Rains
really a support, or isn't his irony—now as famous as Rick's commitment—just
as vital to the movie as the song, the airport at the close, and all that talk about
a hill of beans?

Rick does all the right things—and walks away into the fog with Louis,
the Rains character. Love is being able to dream about it forever, instead of
actually turning it into an everyday reality. So the song fits the "same old
story" of desire being the lasting light.

**" . . . are you falling in love with the person
or are you falling for the past . . . ?"**

LAURA

1944, OTTO PREMINGER

Gloomy Rapture

Laura Hunt is dead. We see her in flash-backs when she was a pretty girl on the make and on the rise in New York advertising. She was Gene Tierney, and she dressed better and picked up smoother manners once Waldo Lydecker (Clifton Webb) took her on as his protégée and his beard. But Laura Hunt is dead, shot in the face with a shotgun. She was a mess. Mark McPherson (Dana Andrews) is the detective on the job and for thirty minutes or so he prowls around the old life of Laura, examining her unappealing friends and being gradually affected or impressed or impregnated by the atmosphere of Laura. This is what Otto Preminger could do.

We know nothing about McPherson except that he smokes and chews gum in Laura's apartment and he has a silly game, based on a baseball diamond, where you have to get silver balls to sit in the holes. He is morose, a little sluggish—or is it depressed? He gives hints of being a pretty good, professional detective, but it's hard to miss his own incompleteness or unhap-piness. It makes him faintly hostile to everyone he meets, and Andrews's lazy Southern speech suits the character.

OPPOSITE: *If you look at a picture long enough, it gets under your skin. Even if she's dead.*

73

And then, about thirty minutes into the film, McPherson elects to spend the night in Laura's apartment. There are several rooms—notably, a salon and a bedroom—and a lot of expensive antique furniture with silk lampshades. It's classy and feminine and the way Andrews or McPherson walks around in it tells us he has some contempt for the place and some yearning. He could tell himself he is looking for clues, of course (and there are clues in the apartment), but it's clear that he is trying to conjure up the feeling of the dead Laura. The scene is actual, factual (detective on the job), but it is mythic, voyeuristic, too—it's a man falling in love.

There's music, too, a tune called "Laura" written by David Raksin, and it's a record on the turntable in the apartment. Once established, it can come in at odd stealthy moments, and in different arrangements depending on McPherson's gloomy rapture. There are mirrors in the apartment—why not? She was a beautiful woman—but they keep showing McPherson his drab self, and that leaves him angry. He drinks her liquor and he sits at her desk, goes through the drawers and tosses bundles of her letters and her diary around as if they were stolen cash and he was the robber.

There's a picture on the wall, a portrait of Laura, done in what you'd have to call a chocolate-box style, and in McPherson's long gaze you feel he might want to eat it. Then Waldo Lydecker appears from out of the night—he wants some of Laura's furniture back. It was his, he says, and he only loaned it to her. But he tells us something he has learned: that Mark wants something, too—the sour detective already has put in a bid for the portrait of Laura. We are not surprised. The necrophilia was there in the helpless way the detective moved about the picture, like a fly in its space.

Lydecker withdraws and McPherson is left alone. He sits in Laura's armchair, drinking still, and he begins to read her letters. The camera sucks in on a close-up as he slips into sleep or dream. The liquor bottle is as large as his head. Then the camera backs away and we hear a clicking sound. The door to the apartment is opening. A figure in white stands there. It is awfully like Laura Hunt.

And this is just about five or six minutes in a film called *Laura*.

It was made in 1944 and it was Preminger's breakthrough. It's of unusual interest in that he was originally just the film's producer. Yet one way and

"The camera sucks in on a close-up as he slips into sleep or dream."

But she's alive: Dana Andrews wakes up to find a living Laura (Gene Tierney).

another he persuaded Twentieth Century Fox that the assigned director—Rouben Mamoulian—was not quite up to it. So Otto horned in on the story, just like McPherson. *Laura* is intriguing, too, in that it's a film made in the middle of the war which simply refuses to admit its existence. This is normal or ordinary love, envy, terrible desire and luxury apartments. Yes, the mystery of who killed whom will be settled, and good luck if it's what you want. But here for a few minutes a director discovers his métier and fills the screen with furtive life.

MEET ME IN ST. LOUIS

1944, VINCENTE MINNELLI

A Family Album

"It has a momentous story."

Anyone who loves movies, and who treasures the musical, has felt troubled that so many of our best musicals were indifferent to story or drama. Who can remember what the Astaire-Rogers pictures are "about" apart from their own rapture of movement and melody? But there are exceptions, films so intriguing in their content that they remind us that all dramatic films have enough musical accompaniment to partake of "the musical."

So Vincente Minnelli's *Meet Me in St. Louis* is a family album and a home musical from the age when families gathered round their piano. It has famous songs, like "The Trolley Song" and "The Boy Next Door." It has a momentous story.

The Smith family live in St. Louis and they are excited about the coming World's Fair—this is 1904. There are the parents, Alonzo and Anna (Leon Ames and Mary Astor). There are four daughters and one son, and there is a grandfather. Quite early in the film, Alonzo hears that the bank where he works intends to promote him to New York. This means an improvement in the family's life and a great change and excitement for the children. So they have very mixed feelings about it. The two older girls have their romantic ups and downs. The youngest has a great adventure at Halloween. And so we come to Christmas.

On Christmas Eve there has been a big dance in town, and after several mishaps and misunderstandings, John Truitt has fulfilled every dream of Esther (Judy Garland) by proposing to her. She comes home and finds her youngest sister, Tootie (Margaret O'Brien), still awake and very worried. Why not? Most kids are pent up on Christmas Eve, but Tootie has other concerns—she doesn't want to leave St. Louis. Whereupon, looking out of an upstairs window at snowmen in the garden, Esther sings "Have Yourself a Merry Little Christmas," music by Ralph Blane and lyrics by Hugh Martin. Is there a more dramatically apt song in an American musical? For this is perhaps the most melancholy Christmas song there ever was. It catches the dismay that is growing in the younger members of the Smith family. You cannot really appreciate or weigh the song without grasping the complex family situation.

Esther delivers the song in a heartbreaking way—you could even surmise

Tootie (Margaret O'Brien).

that this young woman should get to New York fast and go on stage. She may love John Truitt, but is a settled life in St. Louis—like that of her own mother—really her best destiny? Tootie is undone by the emotions of the moment. The little girl runs down to the garden in her nightdress and smashes her own snowmen apart, as if she can only get to New York by destroying St. Louis. Alonzo has just come home and hears the distress. He is lost in thought. There is even a moment when he pauses over a table and picks up a doll—it reminds me of Charles Kane touching the snowball in *Citizen Kane*—and he announces to the family that New York is off. It's not that the bank has changed its mind. Lon has killed his own hopes. He cannot wrench the family away. He cannot face the drastic change and alteration. Tootie's moment means they will stay in St. Louis.

This film opened in November 1944 and it was a huge Christmas hit. Can you wonder? For troops away, for those waiting to see them again, here was a tribute to home (not far from the same theme in *The Wizard of Oz*), that we should trust and abide by home, no matter the savage shifts of war. But this is America! This is the culture that impresses the rest of the world by being based in change, chance and making a brave departure.

I long to see the sequel, in which Lon turns into an alcoholic because he has denied himself his great chance, and Esther goes quietly crazed as a happy housewife and mother. Perhaps that's going too far, but I mean it as a tribute to just how rich and subtle a musical could be. Talking of craziness and the heart's urgings, it was on this film that Minnelli fell in love with Garland, and so they married. It's like smashing your snowmen.

"...we should trust and abide by home, no matter the savage shifts of war."

Two sisters (there are four in the film) wondering whether they will ever get to New York.

THE BIG SLEEP

1946, HOWARD HAWKS

Self-Deprecating Manliness

The private eye comes to the front door—what will he see? What a sight for sore eyes he is. "It was about eleven o'clock in the morning, mid-October, with the sun not shining and a look of hard wet rain in the clearness of the foothills. I was wearing my powder-blue suit, with dark blue shirt, tie and display handkerchief, black brogues, black wool socks with dark blue clocks on them. I was neat, clean, shaved and sober, and I didn't care who knew it. I was everything the well-dressed private detective ought to be. I was calling on four million dollars."

That is Philip Marlowe speaking, and Raymond Chandler writing for him in the book *The Big Sleep*, and that sense of "hard wet rain in the clearness of the foothills" bespeaks a fondness for southern California, but don't forget the "hard" as in "hard-boiled." And don't even ask about the socks and the powder-blue suit. No, this isn't Howard Hawks's Marlowe, not exactly, and Humphrey Bogart dresses like a con just out of prison. But wait, that "and I didn't care who knew it," that's where the two Marlowes overlap. That's what Hawks has understood, and that's the key to this Marlowe. Nothing will shake his romantic view of himself or the self-deprecating manliness.

After that, the opening of the film (even with Jules Furthman, William Faulkner and Leigh Brackett doing the writing) is very true to Chandler. The scene in the hothouse with General Sternwood (Charles Waldron) is all in the book, and the first appearance of Carmen (Martha Vickers), giving the shamus her nympho act and sitting down in his lap while he's still standing up, that's all there, plus Marlowe's line to the butler: "You ought to wean her. She looks old enough."

But then comes the moment, or even the reprise of the moment, for this film is clearly meant as a kind of sequel to *To Have and Have Not*, the film where Bogart and Bacall had met, and so on. So when Marlowe, by now soaked through in his own sweat after the hothouse, is ushered in to see Vivian (Lauren Bacall), Bacall seems very cool, very soigné in satin and long black pants, and maybe half a head taller than the dirty, unwashed private eye who once was sober. A lot of the cross talk in the film comes from the book, but not all of it. In the film, Marlowe has the flick-knife of asking for a drink,

OPPOSITE:

Calling on four million dollars.

81

getting a curt "Help yourself," and then declining it and making her steam. In the book, she tells him off, "My God, you big dark handsome brute! I ought to throw a Buick at you." You can see Hawks wincing at that. Because in the book, Vivian isn't cool and she isn't even very nice, and it isn't going to be a love story or a screwball comedy (as well as a mystery and a noir, and so on).

Chandler had been to an English public school—not the best, but it's at schools not quite in the upper crust that people try hardest. So he had an eye for the hills and the rain and how a man might dress, whereas Hawks needed nothing but talking to women and attempting to be cool. Chandler wrote a mystery story. He seems to have said later that he could never quite fathom it, but I don't believe him. He would try to write serious novels one day and he took his plots responsibly. Whereas Hawks just wanted to get to the stuff where Marlowe and Vivian are so hot for each other that cool insult is their perverse style. We are headed for the telephone scene, don't forget, which is worthy of the Marx Brothers, not to mention the restaurant scene with her in black satin where they talk about horse racing.

It's a treat to go back to Chandler to find what's new and what's different, and there's no doubt that he and Hawks shared a sense of the dreamy calm in the character, a way of taking a beating and still having a wisecrack in your bleeding mouth. But Hawks was uninterested in the story, so long as it allowed a few scenes where a man and a woman could cut each other to pieces and then do a little gentle playing doctor. Which is a mark of his generous spirit, for he must have been a little vexed in that he had always fancied he would have Bacall for himself. To have and have not.

THE RED SHOES

1948, MICHAEL POWELL, EMERIC PRESSBURGER

Natural and Freudian

"...a metaphor for ballet itself, for movie and all arts."

I thought I had this one tidied up. No, I wasn't going to cite the obvious example, the fabulous ballet scene, which is at least twenty minutes of moments. Instead, I was opting for that earlier scene where the impresario Lermontov (Anton Walbrook) begins, "The Red Shoes is the story of . . . ," and in a reverential long shot we see the key members of his company gathering like gazelles at an evening pond. It's not just that the scene so captures the thrall of a dawning project and the exhilarated fellowship of creative enterprise. Beyond that, it is a model of the kind of cooperative venture that the Archers reveled in, under the leadership of Emeric Pressburger and Michael Powell (who wasn't a million miles from a Lermontov).

I ran the DVD to revisit that scene, and it was as delicious as I recalled, and as inspiring, but then, relaxing, I let the tape run and before I knew it, I was plunged into the ballet, at which point I decided I was the victim of my own snobbery and affectation. I had to do the ballet.

The Red Shoes is a brilliant and cunning exploitation of a story by Hans Christian Andersen (scripted by Pressburger) in which a girl craves a pair of red shoes that have a dancing life of their own. The Andersen story ends rather happily but Powell and Pressburger made it a metaphor for ballet itself, for movie and all arts. Powell was quite clear in his calm, fierce way that an artist had to die for his or her art. So their film of *The Red Shoes* is both a fulfillment and an inevitable tragedy, celebrated in color, movement, music, acting, and story.

The members of the Archers company are not just Powell and Pressburger, but director of photography Jack Cardiff (never surpassed in his handling of Technicolor), camera operator Christopher Challis, music arranger Brian Easdale, production designer Hein Heckroth, choreographer Robert Helpmann (who also dances in the ballet) and the other dancers, Moira Shearer and Léonide Massine, plus Marius Goring who plays Julius Craster, the composer and conductor of the *Red Shoes* score.

The ballet we see compressed into twenty minutes must have occupied a full evening in the theater, yet nothing feels missing. How could there be, when the pace and rhythm of the ballet is so demanding? I'm not sure that any real dancer in real time and space could maintain the athletic momentum

OPPOSITE:

Léonide Massine and Moira Shearer.

84

that drives Moira Shearer. The feeling of her being possessed by the blood-red shoes is beyond question; it is passionate, frantic and nearly insane. Thus, the key shots in the sequence may be the amazing big close-ups of Shearer, her face aghast (as if she was uncertain whether she was being adored or ravished), the edge of her hair lit up by flame or a fire that is consuming her. In short, it is a drama, too, as well as a dance, and the moment when the figures of Lermontov and Craster replace the shopkeeper who gives her the shoes are natural and Freudian all at the same time.

Massine is so sinister as that shopkeeper, such a wizard and a demon. I lack the expert knowledge to say whether Ms. Shearer was a great dancer. Suffice it to say that in this extended rapture she is a great actress, driven by the tempest of dance. Whether flirting with the paper figure, whirling from one gaudy partner to another, or the limp rag carried away after death, she is the center of it all, and her performance is so unbridled and compelling that it comes nearly as an afterthought to see that she is dancing.

When this masterpiece was played to its financiers, the Rank Organization, the money men—J. Arthur Rank included—stalked away in bewilderment and hurt. It was rubbish, they said. No doubt they wore the best black shoes money could buy.

"...a great actress, driven by the tempest of dance."

THE THIRD MAN

1949, CAROL REED

It's Over

A graveyard in Vienna: Joseph Cotten and Trevor Howard.

Where do movies go when they end? Once upon a time, if you were technically inclined, the last strip of celluloid snaked through the projector and flapped around on the take-up reel, until that weight of film was lifted out and rewound so that the last reel of *The Third Man,* say, could

be put to rest in its can—until the next show. Movie has always been a physical commodity and a technology as well as a fantasy. The astonishing life we have just seen—the moment—is just a matter of sequential still frames, back to front and upside down, that find their life when set in motion between a shuttered lens and a burning light.

There is another way of looking at the end of *The Third Man*, and other questions to ask about where it goes. At last, on a black-and-white winter's day they have buried Harry Lime (Orson Welles) in the hard ground of Vienna. This time there's no question; premature and evasive funeral announcements are done with. Harry is dead. He gave his old friend Holly (Joseph Cotten) the nod and we heard the gunshot echoing through the sewers. So we make the picture's third trip to the cemetery.

Holly has a lift from Calloway, the cop (Trevor Howard), and as they

"...the picture's third trip to the cemetery."

drive back to town they pass Anna walking. Without much hope Holly asks to be let out to wait on Anna. Holly had fallen for her, but Anna (Alida Valli) was always Harry's girl and she thinks that Holly betrayed his old friend and then had him killed. In fact, he did it to clear up the mess over Anna's papers. But she's not impressed. She always knew there would be betrayal.

So Holly leans against a cart on the edge of the frame. The camera is in the center of the drive looking toward Anna's remorseless approach. Will she stop to speak to him; will she look at him; or is it all hopeless? The zither theme music by Anton Karas builds, but it is more plangent than romantic— nothing in this music encourages our hopes. Still, if Anna comes all the way she will walk into the camera. That feels impossible or awkward. Perhaps she will relent.

But what do we want? Do we really believe Holly and Anna can save each other or will the memory of Harry become quick lime for their union?

Director Carol Reed does not cut away from the single setup. He does not give us a close-up of Holly hoping, or Anna wondering what to do. She keeps coming on.

And past the camera without altering her stride or her resolve. It's over— their fleeting romance and the whole film. Time to go home.

In the old days, this last shot acquired another providential quality. Coming at the end of a reel, the shot suffered in old prints—there were specks of dirt, scratches and blemishes. Traditionally, we expect "perfect" prints, every shot and frame, but this moderate and unavoidable acne of the conclusion to *The Third Man* gave it an extra pathos—it was as if the material itself was weeping or aging. There's a lesson here: The "correct" image in a movie is one thing, but film is artifice, artificial and an art-work, and there is no reason why extra eloquence may not come with degradation.

Still, in 1949 this counted as a body blow to "happy ending" culture, in a movie known for its bleakness about friendship and Europe after the war. So I have to tell you that Graham Greene who did the script, later published *The Third Man* as a story, and there that rigorous and none-too-optimistic author allowed that he suspected the two people paused outside the cemetery, did talk and even walked away hand in hand.

Well, in life perhaps—people are weak and opportunistic there. But you'd like to think a tough-minded author could appreciate his own movie. I think Holly and Anna have to be on their own, and I doubt she will trust anyone again. Holly? Dead from drink in ten years?

"Where do movies go when they end?"

The end of the story: just keep walking.

WHITE HEAT

1949, RAOUL WALSH

Sanity Explodes

In the years after the Second World War the movies cautiously (yet spellbound) turned to our disturbed minds. This was a result of shell-shock during the war, and it would be encouraging to think that writers and directors were moved by the many varieties of madness on display during the war. There was also the fact that plenty of refugee analysts had come to Los Angeles and found clients in the great collection of narcissists, neurotics and fantasists called the industry. So film noir had a lot of deranged characters and in *The Snake Pit* the very wholesome Olivia de Havilland went to the "nuthouse."

Then there is Cody Jarrett, the means of James Cagney's return to the gangster picture. Cagney was reluctant about going back to his 1930s violence—so he said—and in the war years there had been a lot of guilt over gangster pictures because it was felt they hardly presented America in a positive light. But next to George M. Cohan in *Yankee Doodle Dandy*, Cody Jarrett in *White Heat* may be the best thing Cagney ever did. And, finally, neither of them is what you'd call normal.

Cagney was fifty when *White Heat* came out, but Cody is an infant. This is felt all the more strongly because he has a mother, Ma (Margaret Wycherly, who was only nineteen years older than Jimmy). Some writers have said Cody has an Oedipus complex, but that's not the case. He doesn't want to sleep with Ma; he wants to return to her body. He needs to be looked after. So in the famous scene where he curls up on her lap, we are seeing infantilism let loose.

But the moment, the operatic set piece, has Cody in jail, worrying about Ma. The guys are in the mess hall, eating, and Cody passes a message down the line, "How's Ma?" The director Raoul Walsh tracks along several haggard faces until we come to the newest inmate who has the word—she's dead. At which point, the track reverses and the convicts who pass on the dire news are worse than haggard. They know that Cody's uncertain sanity is about to explode—and this is a film about explosions, surely aware of the big bang at the end of the war.

When the news reaches Cody we are ready for something colossal. Cagney begins to moan and grunt. He goes into a frenzy, but he remembers that he

"He doesn't want to sleep with Ma; he wants to return to her body."

93

"...a terrible metaphor of physical and mental confinement..."

was a dancer once and he generates an energy that is both tormented and balletic. The scene was apparently shot in one morning in the studio machine shop—Warner Bros. had wanted to do it in a chapel—and of course it involved a lot of extras and a big space.

Cagney becomes demonic, yet every move is thought out—not controlled but driven and inspired. It counts as an action scene, and a terrible metaphor of physical and mental confinement, but it is an explosion, too, and more than sixty years later it scarcely has a rival for its expression of madness. The film is not over, and we may marvel that Cody is able to put words and plans together in what follows. But as a growing gang of guards is required to restrain him, we are watching something as fully committed and as life-fulfilling as Astaire doing a great dance routine. When Cody is taken away at last, a silence falls on the other prisoners—and we share in their awe. I doubt any actor today would dare to go to the limits that seemed natural to Cody.

At the end of the picture, Cody is shot to pieces on an exploding gas tank and he utters the last cry to his only real companion, "Made it, Ma . . . Top of the world." In being incinerated Cody lived and died by the codes of censorship: So long as you die, you can do almost whatever you like first. But in saving his greatest frenzy for the loss of his mother, Cody and Cagney went a long way to building the perverse system in which we love our movie monsters.

RIGHT: *"Made it, Ma! Top of the world!"*

Love and Contempt

I love the opening of *Sunset Blvd.*, the views of that great wide street as the dawn comes up, the howl of police cars, and then the sight of them racing towards "action." And it seems a part of that noir mood that there's a knowing male voice telling us what to look at—low, dry, an insider, not sentimental and not quite cynical, because after all this is Sunset, a famous street in a city pledged to fame, as well as the section of it where the mansions have enough surrounding ground so that neighbors might not hear a shot or a scream.

Voice-over has gone out of fashion nowadays. Maybe it's too directly linked with storytelling for our comfort. But this is one of the best voice-overs in a field that has a lot of competition—just think of *The Magnificent Ambersons*, *Letter from an Unknown Woman*, *Kind Hearts and Coronets*, *All About Eve* . . .

Why do I love voice-over? Well, it's a way of delivering so much information as well as a key character very quickly. Not that the voice needs to be telling the truth or the whole truth. But it's also because a voice-over reminds me of two other things I cherish: radio and writing. A voice-over needs written words and a great voice.

I should add that the voice-over in *Sunset Blvd.* was meant to be Montgomery Clift. Now, I like Clift, but I can easily imagine, given the circumstances, that his voice would have been plaintive and sad, whereas this voice

PREVIOUS SPREAD:
Every house in Beverly Hills should have a pool. The corpse in the pool is optional.

BELOW: *A screenwriter is dead. But he's still telling the story.*

is relaxed—easy come, easy go. He likes a good story but he isn't going to fall for it. Once Clift knew the dramatic set-up, he would have been hurt—you couldn't ask Monty Clift to be dead, and talking still, without some quaver in his voice. Whereas, Joe Gillis, our voice, is dead. And by the end of the opening there he is floating face down on top of Norma Desmond's swimming pool—and still talking to us.

That's the moment when you knew that Billy Wilder (the director and co-writer) was doing something new and wicked. The story goes that at an early screening of the picture, the great Louis B. Mayer, the head of MGM (just—he was fired a year later) slapped Wilder in the face for treating Hollywood so shabbily. But the truth is over sixty years later, few people know or care who Mr. Mayer was while Sunset Boulevard (the place, the picture and the musical) are emblematic.

I suppose in 1950 some people in the audience were shocked that a dead person was telling the story. But we were innocent then. We hadn't quite appreciated how much the magic of the movies had to do with separation from reality, the life-like absence of life, and death (the first time I saw a James Dean picture, the guy was dead already). Wilder was saying, Look, it's a movie, and movies are crazy, as wild as dreams—that's why this picture is about a movie star who has gone mad, but who will be reunited with the camera, her great lover.

The secret to Billy Wilder is his mix of love and contempt for that world. He had arrived from Berlin and Vienna in the 1930s, broke and with poor English. Then he rose in the fake heaven he found and years before his death he sat in his Beverly Hills office with a row of six Oscars, decrying a stupid industry that would not hire him any longer. He had become a kind of Norma Desmond.

Anyway, Montgomery Clift ducked out of the part because he felt it would be bad for his romantic image to play the kept man of an older woman. Thank God. Because that meant William Holden could play the part and I hope I've persuaded you that he is vital to the sour joke of the whole film. Holden, it seems to me, was in the line of Bogart, and maybe as good. From *Sunset Blvd.* to *The Wild Bunch*, he was superb as a guy who wanted to believe but who had been born a few pounds light when it came to faith. When you hear him start to tell the story of *Sunset Blvd.*, and when you see him dead in the water, but not swallowing water, you're in touch with one of the finest dry, ironic voices in American culture (including Mark Twain and Jack Benny).

"A voice-over needs written words and a great voice."

It might have been Mary Pickford and Montgomery Clift, but Gloria Swanson and William Holden own the legend of Sunset Blvd.

THE RIVER

1951, JEAN RENOIR

Garden Meets Jungle

Jean Renoir's *The River* has dated in several ways. Its view of a middle-class English family existing contentedly in a Bengali garden can strike new viewers as quaint and unduly privileged. Young women of today (and old men) may sigh when Mother tells her daughter, Harriet, about the blessing of having a man's child because it is "a precious, sanctified work," "the meaning of a woman." These things come from Rumer Godden's 1946 novel and if they are accurate to a period and a colonial class that may not be something to take pride in.

Still, it is Renoir in India, in Technicolor, rediscovering passion for film and his confidence after the war and an awkward period in America. The great director rose to all the challenges and if the sentiments voiced in *The River* are sometimes bald and vulnerable, the cinematic vision is wondrous.

The father manages the local jute factory. He is a secure, amiable, limited man (Esmond Knight) while his wife (Nora Swinburne) is lovely, adoring and unquestioning of all she has been taught. They are British India and fond parents who might drive you mad. Lord knows how their children will turn out, but one of them will not leave the garden, which is surrounded by jungle and the river. There are five girls and a boy, and another child is on the way.

The boy, "Bogey" (Richard Foster) is a helpless outsider. Though he seems to bear no grudge. What can he do with so many sisters? So he has found a pal, an Indian boy, Kanu, and in the course of the film we see that they have discovered a snake, a cobra. Where garden meets jungle, they are getting too close to this threat, and they are warned not to go further.

The lure of the cobra.

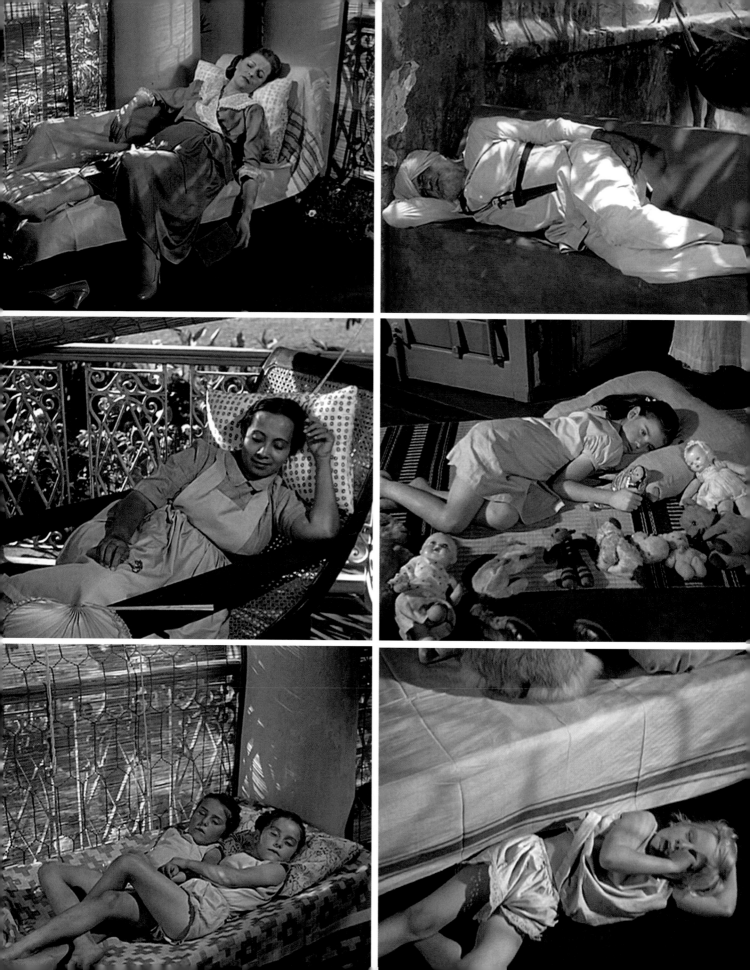

Then comes our moment: It is a hot afternoon and everyone in the household is taking a siesta. There is a ravishing shot of the mother in a mauve dress falling asleep on a yellow chaise longue, and as she drifts off the book she was reading slips to the floor. We see two Indian servants, stretched out or curled up in sleep. We see the children, one with her dolls, two sleeping together, and one girl in her white underwear sleeping on the floor so her pet rabbit may have the bed. The domestic detail is ordinary and heartfelt, and as these shots dissolve from one to another so they are carried on gentle tracking movements, in and out, like sleep's breathing. This effect may not be noticeable at first, but it is palpable and it is a sign of Renoir's love of momentary, organic existence and experience.

A flute plays in the background, and it seems like the music of reverie, but it might be the little boys trying to charm the cobra. And when the flute stops suddenly that wakes Harriet so that she knows something is wrong. She sees Kanu and calls to him, but the boy runs away. So she goes to look for Bogey. She picks up a dropped flute and then she finds the body of her brother. I don't know whether a cobra's bite can kill so quickly or so thoroughly. Perhaps you have to believe in cobras.

So Bogey is gone and the new baby is another girl. It is a tragedy, but it is commonplace. Renoir said later that being in India had brought him calm, so that he could contemplate being a bum for the rest of his life. It didn't come to that. He would go on to make his late masterpieces—*The Golden Coach*, *French Cancan, Elena and the Men*—all of them in color and all filled with the tranquillity that sees life coming and going just as the river flows by. Of course, that feeling had been there a long time if you recall the French river in *Partie de Campagne* (1936), a dappled meeting place for lovers one year and later ruffled by the rain of sadness.

A PLACE IN THE SUN

1951, GEORGE STEVENS

Long Shot

What is the sun, and why do those who live beneath overcast skies long for a place there? Such a question goes to the heart of the mystery of American movie romance, and its effect on us. The movies were a medium that whispered to the masses, "You have a chance, a long shot, but let's make it feel tempting." And so democracy met gambling in the tacit fantasy of advertising. Don't you deserve a place in the sun? Is it in the Constitution? If not, what is that talk of pursuing happiness?

George Eastman is the distant, impoverished member of a wealthy family. He was raised by his mother, a devout and strict woman who ran a neighborhood mission in a city slum. But he wants his place, and his chance rests on looking like Montgomery Clift. George goes west, he gets an ordinary job in a shirt factory that belongs to the Eastman family. There he meets a girl, Alice Tripp (Shelley Winters). Is "Alice Tripp" a warning name? They have an affair. She will get pregnant. But then he is invited—in a patronizing kindness—to a party at the Eastman house. He decides to go. We feel the allure and the danger, and we sympathize with George in his plain suit when so many of the male guests are wearing evening dress. How can he possibly make it to the sun?

His moment arrives in one of the great dreamy meetings in film. Unable to find anyone to talk to, he takes refuge in a room given over to a full-size pool table. He picks up a cue and starts to play. You may wonder how a young man raised in a church mission got so good at pool, but he is masterly—it is his first prowess in the film, beyond looking like Clift. As he plays, a young woman in a white dress pauses in the open door to watch. She is Angela Vickers (Elizabeth Taylor). When they shot the film, she was eighteen, which is indecent, yet it is the movies. She watches George's elaborate cannon shot and as the ball finds its pocket, she breathes, "Wow!" Fate has found its pocket, too.

The two young people talk (though Clift was thirty). Their characters slip into love with the speed necessitated by movie running time. Bit by bit, George abandons Alice. He is infatuated with Angela for herself, and there is palpable chemistry between Clift and Taylor, a fond friendship that lasted until his death and should have made for marriage if Clift had not been so uncertain

OPPOSITE: *Shelley Winters and Montgomery Clift: regular romance.*

about his sexuality and so much else. But Angela represents a better life, a big house, wealth and the sun. Clift is perfect for this role: handsome but weak. It's not long before he considers murdering the awkward Alice.

This story is adapted from Theodore Dreiser's novel *An American Tragedy* (published in 1925), which makes more of the Alice figure—her name in the book is Roberta Alden, surely classier. But the situation that follows, where George thinks of drowning Alice in the secluded Loon Lake, owes a lot to *Sunrise*. The film wavers: It shows George undecided about murder and then it has Alice dying in an accident. Then it cheats again, by having George admit that murder was in his heart. He goes to his death after being found guilty.

The kiss, done with a telephoto lens: Elizabeth Taylor and Montgomery Clift— a smooch in dream history.

Shelley Winters was nominated for a Best Actress Oscar, and she is faultless in a thankless part that impedes the sweet dream we are clinging to. You can say that George is rebuked for his weakness and betrayal, but the film is not called *An American Tragedy* and its title is not ironic. In truth, it is a great thwarted dream—which does not detract from the energy or the passion of the dream or the felt fact that Alice is marginal to the central love story (Winters was required to be dowdy and plaintive by director George Stevens). One "Wow!" and we can be lost. There are few films that tell us more about the ambivalence of the American movie.

STRANGERS ON A TRAIN

1951, ALFRED HITCHCOCK

Criss-Cross

Bruno Anthony is disturbed from the start of *Strangers on a Train*, no matter that Robert Walker trades on his rather plump boyishness, his eager, imploring voice and his admiration for Guy Haines (Farley Granger) the top tennis player. Still Hitchcock loves beguiling talk (which is Bruno's game) and is very unimpressed by athleticism. So it's Bruno we're drawn to, no matter that we can tell he might be dangerous. He has nothing else to do in life. He is so badly but expensively dressed. He's as much a loose end as a silk scarf waiting to strangle someone. And he has the cutest ideas—like criss-cross: you do my murder and I'll do yours.

So we can see that Guy thinks Bruno is foolish, but we know that very opinion proves Guy is the idiot. Then, when we've met the odious slut of Guy's estranged wife—Miriam (Laura Elliott)—well, do I have to tell you more? You see, the people who go to movies, no matter how gentle and law-abiding in their deepest souls, are quite ready to see a murder if it's done with style. (It was Nabokov who said that you can always count on a murderer for a flashy style, and surely that insight comes from the dark of seeing movies, and from his own brief encounter with Hitchcock.)

That's why Bruno goes to Medford, the town where Miriam lives, and follows her to the fairground as darkness falls. And Bruno is such an act: When a little boy brandishes a balloon under his nose, Bruno bursts it with his cigar—the kid cries, but we laugh.

Miriam notices him watching her: she's smart but greedy and she smells money on him. She has local boys with her but she gets rid of them easily enough and then it's the tunnel of love and the island in the evening. Bruno will be her date for the night. We don't like Miriam. No one does. And we're not going to mind her being punished. But part of the fun in his pursuit is the sinisterness and the odd delicacy that descends on Bruno—he does have a purpose in life, something he's good at.

OPPOSITE ABOVE: *Strangers on a train: Guy meets Bruno. Criss-cross. Farley Granger and Robert Walker.*

OPPOSITE BELOW: *Bruno tracks Miriam at the funfair. But where does the tunnel of love go?*

If those spectacles fall off, then the camera could see your murder through distorting lenses.

With fairground music in the distance—mad but jolly—he lays hands on her, not with gentlemanly romance, but with a strangler's grip. She is amazed. She goggles. She struggles. Her glasses fall off and they crack. And here is the moment, for Hitchcock has us see through the cracked lens as Bruno very gently lowers the limp body of Miriam and places it in our laps as we look up at such a gift for our dreams. "There," he seems to say, and the movie whispers it with him, "you know this is what you wanted." You see, it's not just Guy who will benefit from Bruno's loony criss-cross. It's us. We came for a corpse—and we may not be satisfied with just one.

No one in movies had been as mad and nice as Robert Walker is as Bruno, though it's easy to see Norman Bates following along in his steps in *Psycho*. This kind of disturbed but hushed need for violence, this polite cruelty, is one of Hitchcock's most profound discoveries in cinema, just as he was a master of shocking violence done with such craft and dainty meticulousness that it's like a dance. Robert Walker died soon after *Strangers on a Train*, far from the happy man, which was exactly what Hollywood had tried to make of him. People say, "Just think what he might have done if he had lived." But in truth he was uncastable except in the gaze of a Hitchcock. So Guy Haines now looks like a throwback to the worst kind of "Anyone for tennis?" from the theater of the 1920s. But Bruno Anthony is playing a much more interesting game. It's a version of Clue where we did it in the dark just by watching and hoping.

" . . . people who go to movies . . . are quite ready
to see a murder if it's done with style."

TOKYO STORY

1953, YASUJIRÔ OZU

"Make Way for Tomorrow"

The father and mother live in Onomichi, near Hiroshima, a long train ride from Tokyo. But they are elderly and time is passing. They have two grandsons in the big city and they would like to see how they are growing. So they make the journey for a visit, and on the surface it is handled politely and decently, but the film lets us see that the son (a doctor) and the daughter (who runs a beauty parlor) are just too busy to take care of the old people. So the grandparents sit upstairs in their hot room too much of the time, and only their widowed daughter-in-law (Setsuko Hara) really shows an interest in them. Then the grown children have a brainwave: They'll pool their resources and send the parents to a resort hotel in Atami, on the sea, for a few days. It will give them something to remember. It will occupy them and give a reason for the visit. So they make that journey, too.

The grandfather is played by Chishû Ryû, who was only forty-nine at the time. He could pass for much older, seventy perhaps. He is very thin, stooped, gray-haired and with a shuffling walk as well as a slowed but amiable way of grunting or sighing at what people say to him. He has heard so much before. The grandmother is played by Chieko Higashiyama, and I don't know how old she was, though her character is said to be sixty-eight. In 1953, in Japan—which is plainly an impoverished and limited country still, with living space at a premium—this was old age, and old age is a subject that young America sentimentalizes or ignores, no matter that it gathers an increasing "senior" population.

Atami is lovely in its way. It has a cliff sprinkled with trees and a sea stretched out in the sun. But the resort hotel is busy. All the guests wear the same clothes so that it begins to feel like a prison. And in their hot room, the grandparents have trouble sleeping because of the wedding party downstairs, with music, laughter and late hours. It would be easy here for the director, Yasujirô Ozu, to make the older people victims of a crass bunch of kids. But he doesn't do that: The young people are ordinary and decent, and the grandfather especially is seen to be grumpy and difficult. He is old and to the rest of the world that can seem tiresome, and lingering. It's not unnatural.

> **"These children are not wicked; they are pressured by life…"**

OPPOSITE: *Ozu's way of seeing people—still, calm, at a distance—is the essence of his work.*

The parents reconsider.

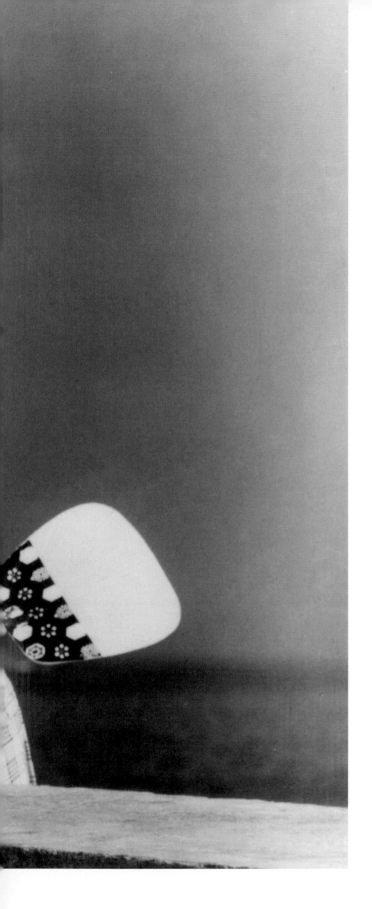

The next morning at Atami, the grandparents sit on the seawall beholding the tranquillity of the sunlit sea. It is the most conventionally beautiful scene in the film, and Ozu places them as distant figures content with the ocean and the light and the peace. But they agree that they are not exactly wanted in Tokyo—that is the Tokyo story—so they will go home to Onomichi. It suits them better. Then as they make to leave, the grandmother has to kneel for a moment. She is dizzy. She is overweight and sixty-eight. The husband is solicitous but neither of them is given a close-up for anguish. We do not even see the woman's face: It is an aspect of this culture that she keeps her pain or fear to herself.

This is far from the end of the film, yet the end has been made clear, and there is nothing to be done about it. These children are not wicked; they are pressured by life, and it is natural that the elderly have to "make way for tomorrow"—to use the title of Leo McCarey's 1937 film, one of the rare American pictures to look at this issue.

All the books say that Ozu is a great humanist, and it's an easy case to feel. But there's more than that. Ozu films from a low level in very still shots. His camera hardly ever moves, and so movements are held within the frame— people come and go, and the fans flap against the endless heat. You can call this style calm and calming, but it is not without a sense of imprisonment and distress. *Tokyo Story* is too polite or too restrained to admit anger, but that doesn't eliminate it—or the way the grandfather is clearly a potential alcoholic. For too long, we have elected to miss the tacit social criticism in Ozu, probably because in the West we believe criticism should be strident or aggressive to prove itself. So I tell you—this is a great film, among Ozu's several great works, but I feel old saying it.

THE BAND WAGON

1953, VINCENTE MINNELLI

Halting and Then Fluent Motion

In the writing of this book, I have left Fred Astaire until this point in his career, because I suspected if I began too early with him, he might take over so many moments. He is one of those areas of cinema—like Bresson or Mizoguchi, Hawks or Margaret Sullavan—where once you are in it is hard to get out, and even unreasonable. Pleasure is an obsession that hardly needs excuses.

In Vincente Minnelli's *The Band Wagon*, we have a behind-the-scenes story of putting on a show (written or assembled from stock by Adolph Green and Betty Comden, who are represented in the movie by Oscar Levant and Nanette Fabray). Today, *The Band Wagon* seems from out of the past. The MGM musical was nearing its end in 1953, but the end was tumultuous, with *Singin' in the Rain* and *An American in Paris* as well as *The Band Wagon*—and Astaire and Cyd Charisse would do *Silk Stockings* in 1957, in which dance and lingerie defeat Communism. I do not mean to disparage Ginger Rogers by not including her, but if the movie musical was going to move forward, I think it had to reach a depth of story (not necessarily plot) that is missing from the Astaire-Rogers pictures at RKO. (As a compensation, those films kept black-and-white.)

In *The Band Wagon* the impresario, Jeffrey Cordova (Jack Buchanan), wants to do a musical that combines ballet and the regular Broadway conventions, so he rashly brings together Tony Hunter and Gabrielle Gerard, a hoofer and a ballerina—or Fred Astaire and Cyd Charisse. In 1953, Astaire was fifty-four and she was thirty-two (and Fred was worried she might seem too tall). Neither one of them was what you would call an actor, though Fred had dismissed that limitation blithely while Charisse never overcame her awkwardness when speaking. And yet, this film and this number, "Dancing in the Dark," would have been much harder to conceive and deliver with Ginger Rogers as Fred's partner. Why? Because there is a deeper romantic need in this number, and because Charisse always found eloquence and eroticism once she began to move.

Tony and Gaby have been introduced and they do not really get on—they have quite different attitudes to dance and entertainment. But they

know they must make an effort, and so they talk and decide to go for a walk in Central Park at night. I must stress the look of this number. Oliver Smith designed a small clearing in the park with a stone bench and a globe lamp-post as well as a silhouette skyline of buildings, and costume designer Mary Ann Nyberg put them both in white against the blue-black of the night. Fred is in a white suit with co-respondent shoes, while Cyd has a white shirt and a very full and pleated skirt—so that it flows and flowers and makes shapes.

"Dancing in the Dark" was written by Arthur Schwartz (Howard Dietz supplied the lyrics but they are not used in this number), and Conrad Salinger did the orchestration. Guess who made the dance?

It is one of the most tender and dramatic dances in Fred's work in that it is the full coming together of two people who are distant and chilly at first, but who are brought to the brink of love by the act of dancing. It is an extended take, of course, in the imperative Astaire style, and in full figure, with the camera moving to cover the dancers. (Minnelli directed, and he was a unique artist, but I think it's clear that Astaire is the auteur of this and most of his other numbers). It is a dance where the two people begin by being apart, and are only slowly drawn into life movements that pick up melody. Touch or contact come gradually and then move into a rapture of embrace, unified turns and exalting lifts. But the hesitancy before the passion is entrancing and the simplicity of the white figures is akin to ballet. As an auteur, Fred had a very simple code: that dance could solve everything. Was the cinema ever closer to bliss?

"Dancing in the Dark"—a title that says so much about the movies as a whole—is a dramatic moment in the film in which the halting and then fluent motion speaks for that other thing, emotion.

"Guess who made the dance?"

A STAR IS BORN

1954, GEORGE CUKOR

Over the Rainbow

Thanks to Ronald Haver's meticulous book on *A Star is Born* (not to mention his restoration of the picture) we know a great deal about the moment of "The Man That Got Away," music by Harold Arlen, lyrics by Ira Gershwin. In the Moss Hart screenplay (derived from the 1937 version, produced by Selznick, with Janet Gaynor and Fredric March), it was to be set in a "dive," a place where musicians jammed after hours. Esther Blodgett (Judy Garland) is there with a handful of musicians, and she starts to sing, unaware that Norman Maine (James Mason) has sought her out there after she saved him from embarrassment at the big Night of Stars stage show. He was drunk then, but he is sober now and he will fall in love with the way she sings "The Man That Got Away." This was 1953, when Judy was thirty-one and, arguably, sometimes looked a little older. Let's face it, she was hardly the ingénue that Esther is supposed to be in the story.

They started work on the number at Warners on October 20, 1953, with Garland's husband, Sid Luft, producing, George Cukor directing, and Winton Hoch as cameraman. But Hoch (a great man with landscape—he did *The Searchers* and *She Wore a Yellow Ribbon*) resisted Cukor's wish to do the whole number in a single take with a travelling camera. He said it was too hard to light. There was further disagreement over whether to use the Warner wide-screen process (WarnerScope) or CinemaScope (the province of Twentieth Century-Fox), which was superior. So they tested both formats, but first Hoch was fired and Milton Krasner came over from Fox to do the tests. Everyone agreed that CinemaScope was superior, so it was chosen at the expense of some $300,000 spent on previous scenes that now had to be written off.

But Krasner was not available for the rest of the film and so Sam Leavitt was hired. There were still complications with the set, and getting the shadowy presence of the musicians in the way Cukor wanted. But Leavitt was fast and accommodating. In one approach, Esther wore a dowdy brown dress and was passing out coffee to the guys. It looked too mundane. Her hair was redone and she was put in a blue-black dress with a white collar. The color scheme was shifted from brown to dark blue and a scrim was put up between the musicians and the bar behind them that gives a more magical feeling. It should be a romantic scene, though you can see the scrim, if you're not looking at Judy.

In three days at the end of October, Garland did twenty-seven takes of the whole number. It took that long because she was not content to mime to the playback—like most people in musicals. She sang along with it and people on set testified that you could always hear her strong voice over the playback. And it was essentially one long take, so she asked for a fifteen-minute break between takes.

"...you could always hear her strong voice over the playback."

You can argue that this is one of Harold Arlen's great blues songs, and Arlen and Judy had history—he had written the music for a song called "Somewhere over the Rainbow" for *The Wizard of Oz* (E. Y. Harburg did the lyrics). You have to say that Cukor achieved a very sympathetic relationship with Garland. And in the arc of the script, this is one of the key moments. But it's not just Norman Maine who falls in love with Esther. This is one of Garland's monuments in a film that was ruined by cuts and studio fears and which did not permit the comeback Judy had hoped for. But if someone at thirty-one is going for a comeback, you know that the real stress within the film is not so much the birth of stars as what happens to them afterward. The story of Judy Garland is more astonishing and gruesome than *A Star is Born*. But these two shots—of Judy in flight and Mason facing the ocean—are as good a metaphor as you will find for what are called the "ups and downs" in show business. Judy was found dead in a London lavatory in 1969.

"... a film that was ruined by cuts and studio fears ..."

SANSHO THE BAILIFF

1954, KENJI MIZOGUCHI

Empty Circle of Ripples

Once upon a time, from out of the past, a nobleman in Japan is sent into exile from his principality because of his inclination to be merciful. He tells his wife (Kinuyo Tanaka) to take their son and daughter and seek refuge as best they can. But in the dangerous travails of the time, the children are sold into slavery and the wife is made a whore. She longs to see her children again, and once, as she tries to escape, she is punished by her owners by the cutting of a tendon in her foot.

Ten years pass. The son and the daughter are still together in servitude. The girl, Anju (Kyôko Kagawa), has tried to live up to the father's hope of showing mercy and kindness to others, but the son, Zushiô (Yoshiaki Hanayagi), has been brutalized, even to the point of being prepared to brand other slaves on the forehead.

One day, the daughter is spinning in her wretched house when a newcomer arrives, who needs to be taught. Anju learns that the newcomer is from the island where she once lived herself, but the young girl knows nothing of Anju's parents, or what happened to them. Then, as the two women work together, there is the sound of a song, a lament. The camera moves away from Anju and we see that it is the new girl singing. The song is one she learned as a child, in which the singer calls out to two lost children, a son and a daughter, and they are named in the song, and how the mother longs to see them again. The song says that life is such a torture. The daughter realizes that it was her mother singing and she now hears the same song in the air or at the sea shore.

Whereupon we cut away to another shore, where the mother is singing the song, bristling in the wind. That is when she is seized as an escapee and she is crippled.

Not long after that, we see Anju from above and behind walk slowly into a still pond. Her progress sends out circles of ripples. Cut away for a moment, and when we return there is just the empty circle of ripples. She has killed herself. She knows by then that her brother has begun to reform himself, and to live up to their father's code. But he has gone away to look for their mother, and Anju cannot sustain herself in the loneliness that brings.

125

In the West, in the 1950s, Japanese movies were a revelation. They seemed exotic so it took time for us to appreciate their human truths.

This film is called *Sansho the Bailiff*, though that is an arbitrary title referring to a rather minor character. The film is by Kenji Mizoguchi, shot in exquisite natural scenery, with the steady, tracking shots that Mizoguchi preferred and which always place the full human figures in a natural and social setting. There is hardly a close-up in the picture, yet it is as emotional as any film in this book. There is an ending, and I will not spoil it for you. It is there waiting for you, and I think you will find that it fulfills many of the themes in the scene I have tried to describe.

"The song is one she learned as a child . . ."

Mizoguchi's tragic romances are dependent as a rule on separation and loss, and the ways in which he can make feeling travel like the wind or like poetry. Here it is the song, and the whole idea that desire in a movie is always best expressed by separation. It is like the gap between us and the screen, the longing to be there and the impossibility.

That very good critic, Anthony Lane, once wrote about seeing *Sansho* years ago and having been so moved that he has never quite wanted to return to it. For it is the cinema as if Shakespeare had been born to it. You, too, may only manage to see it once, on a screen large enough to reward the texture of the photography—but make sure you do that.

All films are about the way people look at the world.

S A N S H O   T H E   B A I L I F F

LOLA MONTÈS

1955, MAX OPHÜLS

Life in the Circus

At the end of Max Ophüls's *Lola Montès*, the infamous courtesan who has contracted to do a circus-ring performance of her own past, has to jump from a great height under the big top into a small pool of water. It is a dangerous finale; she is ill; she is devastated by both the degradation of the circus, and the cheap travesty of her own love life for the benefit of the masses. Before she makes the jump, she nearly swoons, and the ringmaster (Peter Ustinov), her manager and probably her lover, has to talk her over the edge. He has likely done this many times before. Lola Montès died in 1861 after touring in America. She was about forty.

She makes the leap and survives, and then we see her in a cage, wrapped in towels at the head of a long line of men who will pay a dollar to have a kiss from her. Her face is like a mask. She seems exhausted morally as well as physically, and Ophüls's camera simply tracks out over the long line of waiting men while page boys or circus clowns dressed in red collect the money in pots made in the shape of Lola's head. End of film. End of Max. He died two years later in 1957 without making another film. He was fifty-four.

Ophüls was a master of the moving camera, though not simply as decoration or formal exercise. His every move was linked to the mood of the characters or the imperative of the story. Often he moves with the spirit and hope of a character (like Joan Fontaine in *Letter from an Unknown Woman*). Sometimes, as in the start of Lola's circus act, he circles one way while her dais turns the

At the end of the show, kisses for money.

OPPOSITE: *Martine Carole and Peter Ustinov.*

"...she is devastated by
both the degradation of the circus,
and the cheap travesty of
her own love life..."

other to register the artifice and the trap of the show. In *La Ronde*, the very title of the film speaks for the way love makes a dance pattern out of society, without the participants being aware of it. But he seldom tracks out in a direct line as he does at the end of *Lola Montès*, and there is a potent sense of mortality and finality to it. It is not too far from the fatalism of the ballet in *The Red Shoes* and its intuition that this girl must dance until she drops dead. The performer has given up on the safety, the loneliness, the ordinariness of "real life" as a refuge or solace. She has to act out her own life in tawdry circumstances. As François Truffaut observed, this is a story that could apply to Marilyn Monroe and Judy Garland as much as it does to Lola Montès.

The film is a glory of color and wide screen, and it was an expensive production—enough to ensure its box-office failure maybe. There have always been complaints that Martine Carole was too placid or inexpressive for the lead role. But she was a big star at that time, and it is a part of Ophüls's message that Lola was perhaps not really extraordinary—it was just that people needed to think she was. Still, it could have been Dietrich or Ingrid Bergman in the role; it could have been Judy Garland just one year after *A Star Is Born*. It might even have been James Mason as her ringmaster—and Mason loved Max and made two films with him, *Caught* and *The Reckless Moment*.

I am cheating just a touch, because that last moment means more if you have been through the whole circus act with its pattern of flashbacks to Lola's life and if you have felt the emotional mobility of the Ophüls camera. No director proves the principle more clearly: Motion is emotion.

THE NIGHT OF THE HUNTER

1955, CHARLES LAUGHTON

Dementia and Malice

If you were an ordinary viewer in 1955, and if you were watching *The Night of the Hunter* (not many did) you were growing increasingly uneasy. It hardly mattered to the ordinary viewer that the credits declared that the actor Charles Laughton had directed this film. People didn't think they were meant to read the credits. But what on earth had happened to Robert Mitchum, who was his own and everyone else's idea of a cool, taciturn but pretty reliable hero? He was playing a bogus preacher, with abundant signs of dementia and malice. In fact, Mitchum had volunteered for the part when he heard it described, and he seems to have given Laughton every support. But his character, Harry Powell, is very nasty, yet grotesque and half comic. So the audience could see that he was coming for the stolen money he had heard about, and he had a pretty good, cunning idea that the two children knew where it was—their father had given it to them just before he was captured by the police and sent to the prison to be executed.

So this monstrous preacher comes to the country town where the kids live with their mother (Shelley Winters). He does his trick with LOVE and HATE written on the knuckles of his wrestling hands, and he pitches woo to

"...Harry Powell is very nasty, yet grotesque and half comic..."

LEFT: *This is a film where children must look after themselves.*

OPPOSITE: *The preacher comes to town. Robert Mitchum in the role that released his energy.*

133

"Who had seen that kind of thing before?"

the widow. He marries her. He murders her. And there is this shot of her sitting in her car, dead, on the floor of a lake. Who had seen that kind of thing before?

Soon enough he comes after the children and they escape, and that's when the moment arrives and probably the few people left in 1955 walked out. To this point, the black-and-white film had been shot in real rural locations. But as the children make their escape so the world we see turns into that of fairy tale.

The art direction was by Hilyard Brown and the photography was by Stanley Cortez (who had shot most of *The Magnificent Ambersons*). The film becomes a panorama of artifice, with water and a horizon and animals on the riverbank watching the children as they pass by—rabbits, an owl, a frog,  a fox. Later we will see and hear the figure of Powell on horseback silhouetted on the horizon, eternal in his pursuit.

You can say it is the world as seen and felt by children, who have now lost both their parents, but it is also a primitive, demonic world such as the mad preacher has always inhabited. The whole thing comes from a novel by Davis Grubb, often described as Southern Gothic. James Agee did an adaptation, but Laughton had to do a lot of rewriting.

Help is at hand for the babes lost in the wood in the form of Lillian Gish as a godmother to waifs and strays. Love will come past, but for 1955 this was a movie that suddenly plunged past so many movie conventions to the psychic reality of the Grimm brothers and a very dangerous country where children had to be ready to look after themselves. The undoubted genius of Charles Laughton would never direct another film. He would die only a few years later. Yet today this haunting work may be better known than his Captain Bligh or his Quasimodo.

THE SEARCHERS

1956, JOHN FORD

Unfit for Home

In John Ford's *The Searchers*, a white child has been kidnapped by the Comanche. Years pass. She grows up to be Natalie Wood. But her uncle, Ethan (John Wayne), has been searching for her in those years, and he is accompanied or watched by a half-breed, Martin Pawley (Jeffrey Hunter), who is fearful that the outraged and desolate Ethan means to kill Debbie because she has been defiled. They learn that she is the bride of a chief named Scar.

With cavalry and Ranger support, they raid Scar's camp. Martin gets to Debbie's tent. She recognizes him and seems to admit her white heritage. Whereupon Scar appears and is tidily killed by Martin. Debbie is given no chance to register regret. As she and Martin escape she has no time to gather up any infants. The Texas Rangers arrive and cut down any Comanche they can see, including women and children.

Ethan pursues Martin and Debbie. He knocks Martin aside and goes after the girl. He chases her to the mouth of a cave. She falls over, face down, in the dirt.

There is then a single shot in which we see the pink of her tunic. Ethan comes into the frame, picks her up and—as the camera tilts up, changing its angle, seeing sky and putting emotion in the gesture—lifts her up above his head. Her fists are clenched and raised to fight. Will he destroy her? He looks at her and then lowers her into his arms. He says, softly—and John Wayne had a superb voice—"Let's go home, Debbie." Without a word, her head folds in against his shoulder and he makes a move to kiss her. One shot—utterly beautiful, deeply moving, and a way in which the harsh Ethan learns to understand "family" or "race" or "strangeness." If that's how you want to feel it. But the movie is not quite great yet.

> "... the harsh Ethan learns to understand 'family' or 'race' or 'strangeness.'"

OPPOSITE ABOVE:
"Let's go home, Debbie."

OPPOSITE BELOW:
Natalie Wood, John Wayne and Jeffrey Hunter.

The final sequence begins on the veranda of the Jorgenson house as father, mother and daughter see the trio returning. The daughter runs out to greet Martin. Ethan rides on, with Debbie still in his lap. He dismounts and lifts his niece down. Nothing is said but the Jorgensons take Debbie into the house. The camera backs off ahead of their movement to find the frame that began the film: the bright desert and a mesa in the distance and the rectangle of doorway surrounded by dark.

As Debbie and the Jorgensons go in—as Debbie comes "home"—they become silhouettes against the sunlight. The camera exposure is set for the glare outside, the spirit of the film remains there, in space, with Ethan. He steps up on the veranda, as if to enter, too; he did tell Debbie they were both going home. Yet he falters.

Ethan stays outside, looking in at the darkness and at us. There is a wind and dust. His hat brim is flat on one side and curled up on the other, as if from years of being in the open. Then, still looking in, he reaches across his body with one hand to grasp the other arm. That was a gesture used by the old cowboy actor Harry Carey—a Ford favorite for decades, but dead by then. But Mrs. Jorgenson was being played by Olive Carey, his widow, and Wayne said it was a small nod to her, thought up on the spur of the moment. Ethan looks into the dark home and then uses his own gesture to put a spin on his body so that he steps down from the veranda and takes a few paces out into the desert. He rocks and sways a little, not just as Wayne was inclined to, but as if the stepping down and its feeling had unsettled him.

You can say that Ethan is so much in the life of wandering and searching now that he cannot rest. He will go back to the desert and be like a perpetual nomad, waiting to be found, yet elusive. Maybe one day people will go out in search of him, the way Willard goes up the river to get Colonel Kurtz in *Apocalypse Now*. Searching is a life. But Ethan might destroy himself rather than be found. Just as *The Searchers* is prompted by racist anxiety, so it can't lose an intransigent opposition to the progress it has learned. Ethan is a figure of fearsome, impacted desire who knows he must deny himself. He is not fit for "home." He belongs to the desert.

"... the spirit of the film remains there, in space, with Ethan."

SWEET SMELL OF SUCCESS

1957, ALEXANDER MACKENDRICK

Precise Language

Ignored or treated with horror when it opened, *Sweet Smell* has come to be a revered film, as well as one more sign of how brave and unexpected Hollywood could be in the 1950s when the lights of one mass medium (film) were supposedly giving way to another (television). It's true, at the time, the smell overpowered any sweetness as far as the large audience was concerned. Nevertheless, the film is a mess and I have noticed that if I pick out its DVD some night I am inclined to take advantage of that generous but insidious sub-medium's advantage—I play just "the" scenes I treasure, and I never get to the rest of the story.

So I never believed in Martin Milner on guitar in the genteel clubland jazz quintet (despite the fact that most of them were the real Chico Hamilton group) and I have never had any interest in or sympathy for J. J. Hunsecker's forlorn sister, Susie, played by Susan Harrison. I know that we are supposed to believe that Hunsecker has a perverse and overbearing fondness for Susie in which he allows her no life or freedom. I did my best in 1957, but I gave up a long time ago. For that hypothetical attachment is so much less gripping than the love-hate that exists between Hunsecker and Sidney Falco and us.

The film deserved to be a mess. Burt Lancaster bought a novella by Ernest Lehman. He agreed to take on the Scot, Alexander Mackendrick, as director. And when Lehman fell ill, he hired Clifford Odets to carry on the rewriting. Odets was the right choice and the wrong one. He was a great dialogue writer who had lapsed into intense neurotic unease over himself and the way he might have corrupted his own talent. So he ended up rewriting and retyping only hours or minutes before some of the scenes were shot.

" ... the
love-hate
that exists
between
Hunsecker
and
Sidney Falco
and us."

Over fifty years later, the moment that endures—or the situation—has Burt, in a crew cut and horn-rimmed spectacles, as Hunsecker, sitting at his nightclub table, with his own phone, holding court and receiving the supplicants who are hoping to get into his gossip column. Sitting just behind him and to his right is Sidney, not invited, but not quite dismissed, cunning enough to resist the master sometimes (he declines to light his cigarette), basking in J.J.'s abuse and just waiting for what he knows will come, the moment when he will be necessary in the doing of some dirty trick.

It's this torturous bond that is fascinating. It seemed very novel in 1957, yet I think anyone in any walk of show business knew it was based on that old double act, the boss and the yes-man, and by now it's easier to see that the yes-man is a lover—ask most wives.

The film has great virtues, including the tart dialogue, the rich Tri-X black and white shot by James Wong Howe, and the generally unshocked attitude to a world of well-dressed reptiles. The moment (at the same table) where Hunsecker warns off a senator, his vapid blonde companion (a Grace Kelly type on valium) and her manager, is one of the best put-downs in movie history, in which we relish Hunsecker's precise language as well as his insight. But there's a way in which he's doing it all for Sidney, the guy whose prettiness is so infinite—this is J.J. talking—and whose presence suggests protégé, hired killer and private slut.

Did anyone hear the gay subtext then? I don't know or care, because I think time and again movies can be out of the control of the several people making them. You hear now that Burt could be a little gay, but few actors took such care to protect their male reputation on screen. As for Curtis, he had likely had so many women, but there was not a hint of boredom or fatigue. His stamina would have a lot more.

So there it is: The moment of the film is these two men taking razors to each other, and loving the malice. There is so much more plot, but I prefer not to get into it. As a whole, the film can never answer its own best question: why didn't it know to just fill its time with these two men talking to each other?

"It's this torturous bond that is fascinating."

TOUCH OF EVIL

1958, ORSON WELLES

Friction at the Border

*The Mexican-
American border.
A man and a blonde
in the car. Plus the
sound of ticking.*

I f you mention Orson Welles's *Touch of Evil* in the context of a book like this, a lot of people are going to assume that I want to talk about the first shot, from the dynamite being put in the car through the border crossing and the very big bang that forestalls the first kiss between Charlton Heston and Janet Leigh (as Mike and Susan Vargas). I think everyone relishes that scene, and I actually prefer the original version with the trashy music by Henry Mancini as opposed to the later 1998 version in which Walter Murch replaced it with natural sound and the music of the border. But there's no need to get into that argument—see both versions—because the moment I like the best comes later.

It's actually Scene 277 in the published script, and it's the action in Manolo Sanchez's cramped apartment where the search ordered by Hank Quinlan will discover two sticks of Black Fox dynamite, no matter that Mike Vargas has already knocked over the empty box that apparently holds the explosive. For most of the scene the place is very crowded; those present are Sanchez (Victor Millan), Vargas, Quinlan, Schwartz (Mort Mills), Pete Menzies (Joseph Calleia) and Joe Grandi (Akim Tamiroff). That's far more than the place can hold comfortably, but of course there's a camera and its crew and the sound people, and as the several pages of overlapping talk work out the camera and the people are moving around in so lifelike a way you don't quite realize at first that it's all one set-up, one take.

Whereas, the opening shot lets you know from the outset that this is a tour de force. Welles intended it as a spectacular return to the American screen, and he was proud that all the moves and people could be shot in one night. It's also a brilliant demonstration of the film's theme—about two countries and the friction at their border and in the intermingling of races: Don't forget that *Touch of Evil* (a very erotic film) involves a Mexican married to a white American woman. Admittedly, Heston was not a Mexican actor. Still, the sexual undertones and the overall weight of coitus interruptus—no kiss, no honeymoon, and a wondering whether the sweet Susan has been raped—are very suggestive for a film from the late 50s.

But the scene in the motel room is so backhanded, so casual, so perverse, and so amazingly natural that it has far less of a show-off feeling. On the other hand, it is a perfect diagram of Quinlan's corruption, which is proved before our very eyes and by the unbroken stream of the shot, even though we don't actually see Quinlan plant the two sticks. But the excitement with which Menzies finds them is both touching and hideous, for it suggests a pattern of frame-up that has gone on for years.

So Welles could be showy sometimes, and those who resented him were always quick to use that stick to beat him. But Welles was often content with simplicity—think of the strawberry shortcake conversation between Tim Holt and Agnes Moorehead in *The Magnificent Ambersons*. In truth, the apartment scene is after the style of Renoir, although cameraman Russell Metty likes a glossier, more noir image than Renoir would have chosen. It's a scene in which Welles the maker of edited scenes knows that a single cut would break the logic and the spell. It's theatrical (it's as melodramatic as discovery) but it's naturalistic, too, and it is the first revelation of the fatal conflict between Vargas and Quinlan.

ABOVE: *About the closest Mike and Susie Vargas get to a love scene—a production still. Charlton Heston and Janet Leigh.*

" . . . the apartment scene is after the style of Renoir . . ."

So this was filmed in 1957, when Welles was forty-two—though Quinlan looks and feels twenty years older. But that was a kind of self-hatred in Welles, the urge to make himself as gross and loathsome as possible. Just don't miss the way I shoot film, he says. And he gives us two fantastic moments, one for the kids and one for the mature viewers. All right, "mature" may not be the best word. Let's just say for the people who always knew that Orson Welles could do anything so naturally that—from time to time—he became a little bored.

Add this: The Sanchez apartment scene was the first shot in the entire production. They took all day setting it up and rehearsing, with three rooms and breakaway walls and marks all over the floor. The camera operator was John Russell—a few years later he did the cinematography on *Psycho.* They filmed it soon after 5:30 P.M. And they got it—fourteen pages of script in one shot.

ANATOMY OF A MURDER

1959, OTTO PREMINGER

Unmentionables

"...'panties' are going to be talked about."

The regular judge is away, so a replacement comes to the wintry upper peninsula of Michigan to try Lt. Frederick Manion (Ben Gazzara) for murder. This is what seems to have happened. Manion and his wife, Laura (Lee Remick), are stationed at Thunder Bay. While the husband was sleeping one evening, Laura went to the Lodge. She had some drinks; she played pinball; she showed off her body and her provocative clothes—in short, she behaved like Laura Manion, a woman who admits that men have been coming on to her all her life, and she has done little to stop the flow.

She spent much of the evening with Barney Quill, the proprietor of the Lodge. He offered to drive her home, and in the process he raped her. Laura is quite certain of this—she says a woman always knows—no matter that the police doctor found no semen and admits the great difficulty in determining whether a married woman has ever been raped.

Still, Laura staggered home and told her husband. He made her swear to it on a rosary (he doesn't seem to trust her—he doesn't seem to like her!). About an hour later he took off for the Lodge and shot Quill dead. It sounds like murder. But Paul Biegler (James Stewart), a local lawyer, coaxes the insolent, arrogant Manion into working it out that he must have gone crazy. He killed Quill in a spurt of "irresistible impulse." But will that defense hold, especially when the anxious and rather dumb local district attorney calls in an expert lawyer from the state capitol, Claude Dancer (George C. Scott)?

Now, don't laugh or squirm, don't giggle as if it was still 1959, but a pair of panties are going to come into play. Quill apparently ripped off Laura's panties, and they haven't been seen since. As the trial unfolds, and the matter of the rape is aired out, it's evident that "panties" are going to be talked about. Judge Weaver calls the several lawyers together and in hushed sidebar they wonder what word can be used in court. Biegler says he doesn't know because he's a bachelor—this is one of Stewart's best wide-eyed looks and proof of

Joseph N. Welch: how a lawyer got to be a judge.

Biegler's lack of scruple. The district attorney says he never heard another word from his wife. Dancer admits that he has known a few French words, but they tend to be suggestive. "French words usually are," regrets Weaver.

So the judge breaks the news to the crowd in the court, and they laugh their embarrassed heads off. Maybe in 1959 the movie audience had the same reaction. At which point, Judge Weaver warns us all that "panties" are going to play a significant part in this trial, which turns on two lives—those of the victim and the man charged with the crime. So get your laughing done with and then behave like grown-ups.

Weaver says this, as he says everything, with a calm dignity and intelligence that put him among the most appealing and enlightened judges in the movies. But he is not exactly an actor, unless you believe that every courtroom is a natural theater. He is Joseph N. Welch, sixty-eight at the time of filming, and a lawyer who had risen to heroic status during the Army v. McCarthy hearings of 1954 when (on live television) he had been able to rebuke the senator from Wisconsin, with, "At long last have you left no sense of decency?"

Lawyer's sidebar: Judge Welch talks to James Stewart, the local DA and his very able second, George C. Scott.

Welch had never done a movie, but when Otto Preminger showed him the script he proved his mettle by reading just his own part. He was a natural. So he was cast, and he is as droll and exact as everyone else in this very entertaining picture. But *Anatomy* is also the breakthrough in court films, where we the audience are as much in the dark as any real jury. *12 Angry Men*—only two years earlier—knows what happened in its case and demands justice. *Anatomy of a Murder* says you never know with "justice." The verdict is the score in the game. It's the result, but it may not be correct. Even decency is a matter of opinion. Doubt reigns, and panties should be taken seriously.

"... a spurt of 'irresistible impulse.'"

"How is the laundry handled at Thunder Bay Inn?" Kathryn Grant and James Stewart.

NORTH BY NORTHWEST

1959, ALFRED HITCHCOCK

Perverse Comedy

suspected that if I left this scene out no one would take the book seriously. So allow me to stress at the outset that it is one of the most far-fetched events ever filmed in an alleged drama. Don't forget that the phrase from the title comes from *Hamlet* ("I am but mad north-north-west"), and it alludes to a kind of deliberate madness meant to throw people off the track. One equivalent of that is Alfred Hitchcock's certainty that, if a thing worked on screen, it was unimportant that it might have worked nowhere else.

And so, Roger O. Thornhill (Cary Grant), in his crazed attempt to prove his innocence (a state of being that never worked with Grant's face or bearing), undertakes an appointment to meet the mythical George Kaplan: He is to take the Greyhound bus out of Chicago, headed for Indianapolis, and get off at the "Prairie Stop" on Highway 41. In fact, they filmed the scene in the semi-desert outside Bakersfield, in California, and it feels as hot and unpleasant as that area, as well as ridiculous. Thornhill has the kind of smart gray suit you expect Cary Grant to wear, but nothing else—no luggage, no book to read, no life (no cell phone). He sees a man at the bus stop (the dour, reliable Malcolm Atterbury, uncredited), but he's just waiting for a bus. Still, he does have the local knowledge and the vague story sense to wonder why that plane over there—a gnat in the blue, a snarl on the sound track—is "dustin' crops where there ain't no crops."

Are we in Kansas?
Cary Grant waiting for the bus.

Give a hint like that to Bernard Herrmann and his danger music picks up. And it is a question: This terrain is no more promising as arable ground than the part of Monument Valley where John Ford put homestead farms in *The Searchers*. But now Thornhill does look at the plane and that's all the provocation the gnat needs. With the man off on his bus, attack can commence. The gnat becomes a wasp.

As the plane makes clear its intention of killing Thornhill, where can he hide on the bald prairie—why not in a square of fatuous corn set down on the ground for this very purpose? Not that the contradictions or continuity errors obtrude. The arc of cutting and danger—all tinged with black comedy—is under way.

It is an immense, composed ordeal (Hitchcock and his writer Ernest Lehman worked out every detail before they got to Bakersfield), and proof that Hitch could put anyone through it in the desert as easily as in a motel shower. What's the point? To give us a roller-coaster ride. Within the context of the film it's killing by overkill. If "they" (whoever they are) really wanted Roger removed, the man at the bus stop could be a hired killer. But if the plane has this insistent hostility toward Roger, and we are to remain in the dark, then somehow even if Roger escapes with his suit in shreds but his life intact, the pilot of the plane has to perish. This is accomplished when the plane slams into a diesel truck that comes charging across Highway 41, leading to a very merry and colorful explosion. Whereupon we dissolve back to Chicago so the chase can resume.

Not that *North by Northwest* is mere exercise. Roger starts as a kind of wastrel, fit for the advertisements he makes, a guy ready to pick up with an attractive blonde on a train and sleep with her simply because she's obliging. He never wonders why or takes her seriously until he realizes he's in love with

"What's the point? To give us a roller-coaster ride."

her. At which point the couple have to save themselves and peril takes on a more intimate form than either Highway 41 or the frozen faces of dead presidents on Mount Rushmore. Everyone said Hitchcock made thrillers, and surely there is suspense here. But *North by Northwest* is an absurdist farce, all done with a straight face and the pounding of Mr. Herrmann. It's one of our most perverse comedies.

Cary Grant and Eva Marie Saint on the presidential roller coaster.

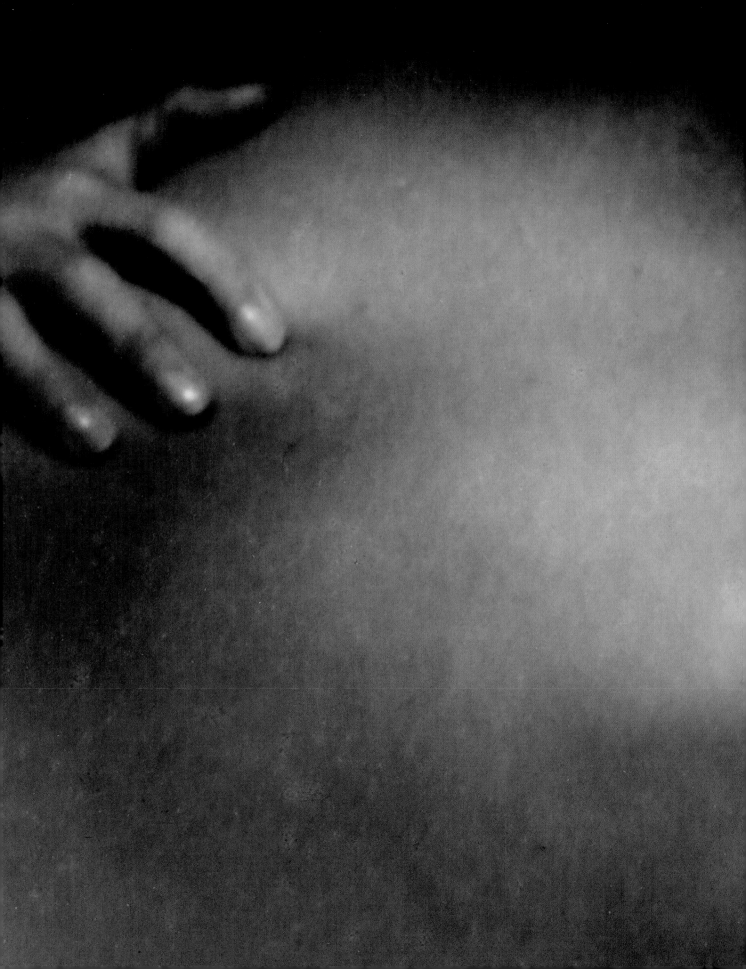

The Heat of the Sun

I n 1959, it wasn't simply a surreal juxtaposition, but political and ecological apprehension, that put Hiroshima and amour in the same title. Alain Resnais had made outstanding documentaries—*Night and Fog* (on Auschwitz) and *Toute la Mémoire du Monde* (on the Bibliothèque nationale de France). This was his first feature, made in collaboration with the novelist Marguerite Duras. And while it looks and feels wondrously composed or balanced in its different juxtapositions, like so many great films it emerged out of a lot of chaos and uncertainty.

I have two moments, and you must forgive me if I say they are linked, but this is a film about love. So the first moment is the opening when we see nocturnal close-ups of parts of embracing bodies, a man and a woman. We never see faces, but we hear the liturgical conversation—she saw things in Hiroshima, she says; no, he responds, you saw nothing in Hiroshima. There is also the haunting, pulsing musical score by Giovanni Fusco (flute and piano) as counterpoint to the words—there are few films that tell us to listen more closely so early.

PREVIOUS SPREAD:
Hiroshima
Mon Amour,
*the opening—
a film about skin and
hands.*

BELOW: *The position of
an arm reminds the
woman of Nevers and
an earlier love.*

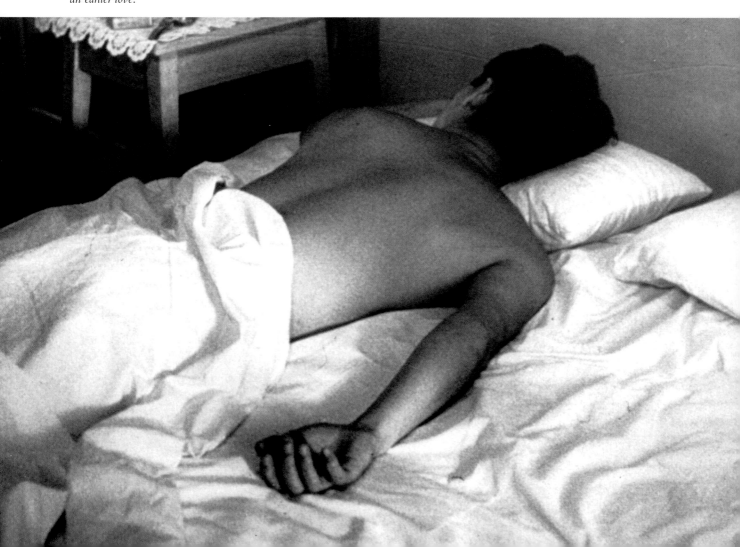

But the bodies are not just flesh. There is an accretion of dust that glitters like gems; it could be debris from some explosion, or the old lava of a volcano, or it might be fallout from an atom bomb, or it could be the sweat of ardent lovemaking on a hot night. How hot can it be in Hiroshima in August? It depends on the exact day in August. One day it was the heat of the sun for a moment.

The eroticism of these shots actually surpasses those scenes in *La Guerre Est Finie* (1966), a more conventional film about lovemaking in which Resnais had the considerable asset of a twenty-three-year-old Geneviève Bujold. Alas, that is like other sex films, especially those with a young girl and a middle-aged man (Yves Montand). The opening of *Hiroshima Mon Amour* is more hot, stealthy and poetic than anything anyone had seen in 1959, and I'm not sure it's been surpassed since. Of course, when a fuller reality set in we saw there was one more juxtaposition—a very striking one for 1959—the woman was French (Emmanuelle Riva) and the man was Japanese (Eiji Okada).

Not too long after this, the bodies of love come into play again. The Japanese man is asleep in bed. The French woman is walking around the apartment and she notices the odd way in which the man's arm is twisted as he sleeps. There is then a cut to the same shape in the arm of her German lover in France during the war, after he had been shot. In a way, it was a Russian cut—like Eisenstein using form to make a narrative leap—but the context was altered by that opening. This is a movie that cherishes the body. In the same way, when the French woman has her hair cropped and her face befouled for being a collaborator, that rhymes with the documentary faces of Japanese people burnt and scarred in the consequences of August 6, 1945.

Alain Resnais has made many more films and some are magnificent—*Providence* (1977), for instance—but I don't think anything has been superior to or more audacious than *Hiroshima Mon Amour*. Equally, this film opened in 1959 which is famously the year of the New Wave breaking on the shore. But it is better than most films made in that great surge of change and hope. *Hiroshima* and *Les 400 Coups* were in the same competition at Cannes for the Palme d'Or (won by *Black Orpheus*!), though *Hiroshima* was withdrawn from competition to avoid injuring American sensibilities. The U.S. tries to believe love and its lovers will not die.

"This is a movie that cherishes the body."

Emmanuelle Riva and Eiji Okada. Over fifty years later, she would be the woman in Amour.

HIROSHIMA MON AMOUR

159

PSYCHO

1960, ALFRED HITCHCOCK

Traps and Traps

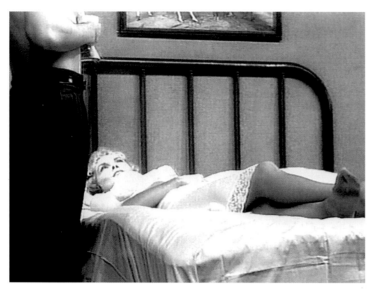

A lunch-hour liaison: Janet Leigh in her underwear—character, actress and hooker?

The most remarkable and affecting scene in *Psycho* comes just before the shower scene. Consider the process: Marion Crane (Janet Leigh) is desirable but thwarted in her desire—she wants to be with Sam Loomis (John Gavin). We see them half naked in the first scene and we know what has happened, but we didn't see it. That hotel room is so sordid and depressing—the whole film is shot in a very harsh black and white, without much prettiness or glamour.

So the scene is a tease and a frustration and it is the first of three scenes in forty minutes in which we will see Marion stripped down to her underwear. The pressure of voyeurism is building. But note in passing how little impressed or interested in Sam Alfred Hitchcock is. In fact, Loomis is one of several abrasive, cold, suspicious, staring people Marion has to endure: the bitch she works with in the office (Hitchcock's daughter, Patricia); the horny client; her anxious boss; the faceless state trooper; the cocksure car dealer. Not a nice one in the bunch and it's all grating on Marion, to say nothing of her long drive, a bad night sleeping in the car, the mounting guilt over the $40,000 she has stolen, and then the rain as night falls. So she stops at a motel.

And that's where she meets the first gentle, sympathetic or insightful person in the film. Now, I will concede that there are some worrying things about Norman Bates (Anthony Perkins). He can lose control all of a sudden

"And that's where she meets the first gentle, sympathetic or insightful person in the film."

OPPOSITE: *Anthony Perkins and Leigh.*

and suffer a surge of anger. He seems to have a very empty life, except for his mother. But Hitchcock is fascinated by him—don't forget Anthony Perkins was the first decision in the casting process—and Marion is sufficiently calmed and swayed by what he says to decide she will go back to Phoenix next day, return the money (or what's left of it) and make amends. She and Norman talk about the traps in life and she sees that she was heading into one. Tomorrow she will go back to her past. Norman may be more deeply caught. His mother seems to treat him very badly. But Norman is as shy, polite and engaging as Anthony Perkins. Despite his solitude, he seems to understand people. This is not just the most absorbing personal conversation in the film, it is one of the most searching talks in all of Hitchcock.

It is set in the parlor behind his office as he asks her to share in a simple cold supper, and it is not a warm or friendly room, not with the stuffed birds on the wall. But Hitchcock films it with great care and a kind of tenderness. People always say the shower scene took a week to film in all its very contrived short, sharp bites. But this supper scene needed much more in the way of writing and rehearsal. And as you watch you may begin to ask yourself, Doesn't Norman look rather like Sam? Except that Norman is nicer.

So there are traps and traps. And just as Hitchcock has laid out kindness, he is preparing for a corpse. We are there as ongoing voyeurs because a part of us has been with the film grilling Marion. We expect our pound of flesh and some blood. Of course, then we are trapped again, because just as once we identified with Marion, now she has been so suddenly removed, who is left to like? Well, Norman is the only candidate in sight and he does seem to be shocked by what has happened and to be determined to do a long, careful clean-up in the bathroom—time for us to settle our nerves and ask ourselves whether there may be worse to come.

"And just as Hitchcock has laid out kindness, he is preparing for a corpse."

OPPOSITE: *The simple supper in the parlor, and maybe the best conversation in all of Hitchcock.*

JULES AND JIM

1962, FRANÇOIS TRUFFAUT

Just Behold Her

As with any period film, François Truffaut's *Jules and Jim* involves time travel. From that ultra-hip French moment of 1961 (when the ties between movie and the world seemed to be shifting, or making love), the film is a quest in nostalgia, going back to the years between 1910 and 1930, to clothes, décor and the antique means of transportation for which Truffaut had a special fondness. Yet now, at about the same distance that separated Truffaut from the era before the Great War, the "newness" of the New Wave looks like a poised wave in a Monet painting of the sea. The moment of insurrection is now classic. But a thing called freshness has survived, and it makes the film as emotional as it is fixed in motion.

Catherine is everything the film, Truffaut and Jeanne Moreau can make her. She is its core and its moment. She is the woman "every" man falls in love with, but while she eats up that affection like a camera absorbing the light, she is never satisfied or convinced. She knows that every split second is a remorseless proof of time. Every screen beauty, every emblem of charisma and caprice, is fading and dying behind their own eyes.

Jules and Jim adore her, they worship her; her odd, alarming modernity is like a god come down to caress their eyes. Jim knows Jules was there first, but everyone and the camera knows that anyone can look at Catherine and be lifted up or damned by her. And so, as the trio go off to the country for one of their sublime and blithely unfinanced holidays, the film simply looks at Moreau being Catherine in a few moments of time. (In the same year, in *La Notte*, Michelangelo Antonioni did much the same thing with the actress, letting her character stroll

" ... there was a time when any director hiring her was resigned to being in love with Jeanne Moreau."

aimlessly on a summer afternoon in Milan, seeing and being seen. Let the actress hold the screen, free from contrived plot or incident. Just behold her.)

So as Catherine reigns over the small group, Truffaut gives her shots and screen time, and every now and then he freezes the frame, as if hoping to say, "Look, this is forever." So in the flood of movie and time there are stills and eternity, with her breezy hair in the wind and herself resolved to be a dream portrait entitled "Young Woman, or Dangerous Beauty."

We fall in love with Moreau and Catherine, and it's plain that Truffaut is slipping the same way. Where else to go? To photograph someone, to say, "Please be still and look that way; think of nothing except your inmost thought," is a twentieth-century way of saying, "I love you—let me watch." Quite quickly, the habit of filming becomes cold-blooded, prurient or only voyeuristic if there isn't affection involved. But built in to the technology of the camera there is the reliability of promiscuity. It's such an easy way of saying, "Aren't they all beautiful? Or magic?" So more or less homely men told beautiful girls they were going to photograph them. The process allowed those shy men to gaze at girls, and tell each one of them, "Oh, you're special, so rare." Whereas anyone who has handled a camera and used it to examine a beloved knows that the technology is only teaching your eyes and guarding your betraying instinct so that you can fall for so many more while telling yourself you're just watching.

There was a time, one by one, when François Truffaut fell in love and into affairs with all his actresses (I think Isabelle Adjani was the only big exception, and she goes mad in *The Story of Adele H.*), and there was a time when any director hiring her was resigned to being in love with Jeanne Moreau. Times have passed. The directors are dead and Mlle. Moreau is eighty-four. She looks it, alas, but she looks so strong still, so fierce toward our timid eyes. She looks like a witch, whereas in *Jules and Jim* we and Truffaut shared the

happy illusion that she was our muse. She was a moment then but she is time now, and much harder to look at. On her own face you can see the dismay she has learned from the mirror. So we are crazy when young about the movies and our photograph albums, but as we grow older looking at that fixed and imprisoned past only reminds us of our life sentence. Time off for good behavior? Don't kid yourself.

Catherine, with some of her admirers, notably Oskar Werner and Henri Serre as the title characters.

THE EXTERMINATING ANGEL

1962, LUIS BUÑUEL

A Very Bourgeois Fallacy

The movie screen has an immense authority. As we look at it, we say to ourselves (or we did, as long as photography prevailed), Well that happened, because "they" recorded it in a system that we know is reliable. That is a matter of fact. But the "fact" was all fabricated. What we are looking at is a record of a pretense. So, there is no great need to make the image or the texture of film dreamlike, or imaginary or "surreal." Keep it as matter-of-fact as you like. Don't bother with losing focus, or adding the wail of distorted violins. Just show us matters of fact, but treat them as models of unreliability. Look at Luis Buñuel.

In the Mexican film *The Exterminating Angel*, a group of socialites come to a dinner party at a fine house on the Calle de la Providencia. There are several courses and there is small talk, and then, gradually, at the suitable moment for departure something odd happens. It is not quite so much a moment or a situation as a vacuum into which the action slips. Without being aware of it at first, or having any reason, the guests do not depart. No, the door is not locked. There are not troops lined up outside with rifles ready to pick off anyone who appears (or not yet). It is not that there is a sublime game of chance keeping everyone in the house. Instead, they face a kind of neurotic negation, an inability to do the proper thing. So they stay the night, and one day stretches into another. They are marooned, almost as if they were on a desert island (Buñuel did make a Robinson Crusoe film). I must stress that while we see and hear a good deal of some of them, they are hardly characters with their individual stories to pursue. They are figures, ciphers, ghosts, and while Buñuel is polite to them, he is not interested in them. Indeed, Buñuel never bothered to care for his people. He realizes there is no point to that sentimentality. Unless you are addicted to sentimentality—and a lot of movies have tried to teach us that habit.

The idea of a band of wealthy people unable to leave the cold site of an old dinner party is comic—though laughter is not expected of us—and it is frightening, too , though Buñuel wants us to be essentially indifferent. Suspense is so vulgar. You could say that we are more required to see the hollowness of

"...they stay the night, and one day stretches into another."

dinner parties, social gatherings and society itself. Buñuel, ever since *Un Chien
Andalou* and *L'Age d'Or*, has taken the attitude that people have to do something
to fill or pass their time—so they eat, they have sex, they lie, they dream and
they gather together like peas in the bottom of a saucepan. This resignation
may not be to everyone's taste. But Buñuel remains one of the greatest of
filmmakers.

The plight of the guests on the Calle de la Providencia is like the difficulty
those other social mannequins have in getting a satisfactory dinner in *The*

Discreet Charm of the Bourgeoisie, or the way in which in *That Obscure Object of Desire* Mathieu (Fernando Rey) cannot tell one Conchita from another—when Maria Schneider had to be released from the role, Buñuel responded by replacing her with two actresses, Carole Bouquet and Angela Molina. This makes a chump of Mathieu, I suppose, but it also helps us see the far more ominous or deflating possibility that all of our partners are alike and unrecognizable. Character is a very bourgeois fallacy, I'm afraid. But we cling to such notions.

BOTH PHOTOS: *As it sinks in, that there is no escaping the room, the guests become inmates, depraved and desperate.*

VIVRE SA VIE

1962, JEAN-LUC GODARD

Swing

Vivre Sa Vie, to live one's life, was Jean-Luc Godard's third film and his first complete commitment to his new wife, Anna Karina. Yet she plays a rather forlorn girl, a would-be actress (that old story) who becomes a prostitute when the creative career falters. There are other versions of that motif in this book—*Klute* and *Lola Montès*—and there are far more films that track the same rueful line. It's not that the movies have ever misunderstood that large sub-text.

The film is in twelve episodes or chapters, marked off by titles, so it's a film made of moments, fragments, aspects or situations. I suppose that authorial control was as much a warning sign to Karina as the fictional destiny that sets her up as a potential actress (much moved by the sight of Falconetti in *The Passion of Joan of Arc*, and sporting a Louise Brooks haircut), but assigns her to the life of a whore and an abrupt demise. So the moment or the chapter that I elect is the one in which Karina and her character, Nana, are given the most liberty and exercise.

By the time of Chapter 9, she is a working whore with her pimp, Raoul (Sady Rebbot). He takes her with him to a café where they meet his friend, Luigi (Eric Schlumberger). While the two men talk, Nana runs out of cigarettes and a young man buys her a packet of Gitanes in what is plainly a romantic gesture and not a professional overture. But this comes after Luigi has entertained her with a foolish but appealing mime act about a little boy blowing up a balloon and having it burst in his face. Nana laughs and then she is charmed by her shy young man and his discreet gift of the cigarettes. The title to this chapter has said, "Nana asks herself if she is happy." Raoul tells her to take care of herself while he and Luigi discuss some matter.

So Nana goes to the jukebox and puts in a coin. As the script says, "Musique bruyante d'un swing endiablé" ("loud swing music"). It's not a piece I ever knew; it's an example of French musicians trying to imitate the American manner, but not rock and roll: "Swing, je t'aime / Swing, tu m'aimes / Swing, je t'aime . . ."

The words are by Jean Ferrat and Pierre Frachet with music from Michel Legrand, but it's not "The Man That Got Away." Never mind. It carries Nana from wistfulness to joy, from servitude to exuberance, as she starts to dance to the jukebox. She dances nicely. But no better than maybe 100,000 Parisian girls might have done. The sweetest thing about this "routine" is that it is nothing like as formal or deliberate as Gene Kelly and Leslie Caron slipping into "It's very clear . . ." in *An American in Paris*. Instead, it's a movie director wondering if his girlfriend could dance to the jukebox, and she says,

" . . . the moment . . . in which Karina and her character, Nana, are given the most liberty and exercise."

"It's your girlfriend doing Cyd Charisse . . ."

Oh, yes, maybe I could do that. She is cautious at first and then the music and her own excitement take her over. It's your girlfriend doing Cyd Charisse—and why not if you sometimes nurse silent dreams of being Fred Astaire?

The dance is as long as the record and there are two ways Godard has of covering it. We see Karina whirling and turning as she dances round the room, and then there is a point-of-view shot—from the vantage of Nana herself—that shows the room passing by, with Raoul and Luigi looking up from their talk to notice her, amused, surprised, touched but just a little dismissive, too. Who does she think she is—Cyd Charisse?

The young man observes her and later they will have a romantic interlude, all too brief before Nana meets her end on a side street. You can argue that *Vivre Sa Vie* is a very composed and gloomy piece, for all its essay-like sections and despite its blithe air of being improvised as we watch. The tart with the heart is doomed. The actress is trapped. But for these moments she gets relief and shows us and herself that she is a lively young woman, as susceptible to life as she is to music. In 1962, it was impossible to see the film without believing that Godard loved Karina. Now, decades later, there is a darker meaning to the film (to be pursued in *Pierrot le Fou*, page 180). Still, on a desert island, I think I'd want that trite "Swing!" dance and the moment when Karina was an icon of new cinema.

L'ECLISSE/THE ECLIPSE

1962, MICHELANGELO ANTONIONI

Were We Really There?

If the movies institutionalized the love story (and our desire for sexual fulfillment) in a mass society, Michelangelo Antonioni is the filmmaker who believes—against his considerable sentimental instincts—in the inevitable dispersal of society, couples and romance. *L'Avventura*, *La Notte*, and *L'Eclisse* made up one of the most deliberate and beautiful trilogies in world cinema. To take on that sort of trilogy project denotes a certain self-importance and gravitas, for which Antonioni was often reasonably mocked. But the trilogy is still, fifty years later, one of the most provocative statements about film as a narrative form.

As *L'Eclisse* begins, Monica Vitti, playing Vittoria, is emerging from an unhappy love affair. She is a translator, and thus an intellectual, but she has an intense vitality or sensuality—as is evident when she puts on a wig and does an African dance in blackface. Then she meets a man, Piero, who is not really her type, a fierce operator in the Italian stock market, played by Alain Delon.

Trying to be wild and free.

SEC MERIDION
RINASCENTE
COTONI
VISCOSA
CHATILLON
FISAC
NEBIOLO
SIELE
AMIATA
MONTECATINI

M MARELLI
VALDARNO
UNES
RO ELETTRIC
SIP
MEDIO PIAVE
SME
SADE
EDISON
SARDA

FIAT
ZUCCHERI
FIAT PRIV
MIRALANZA
ANIC
RUMIANCA
LARDERELLO
SERONO
SARDM

BONIFICHE
RISANAMENTO

CONDOTTE
MARCIA
ITALGAS
LIQUIGAS
PIBIGAS
SIO
TERNE DI ACQUI
VIANINI
MARTINENGO
CEMENTIR
CERAM POZZI
REND 3 50

*Frenzy on the floor of
the stock exchange.*

You feel a marked difference between the two of them, but their bond is arguably the most erotic in Antonioni's work just because of that gap. All too often,
he regarded sex as a process on its way to conclusion or disappointment. His
lovers seldom speak of their need, but here it is palpable.

In *L'Avventura*, famously, one lover vanishes on a trip to an island. In her
absence, another relationship forms, and nearly breaks up. In *La Notte*, the
wife and husband are on the brink of accepting the loss of interest they feel in
their marriage. Then in a bitter dawn they stumble toward reconciliation. But
L'Eclisse goes farther. The unsuitable couple excite each other, and we see the
man's wolfish energy in a fabulous sequence of action on the floor of the stock
market—maybe the most frenzied scene in Antonioni.

Alain Delon and
Monica Vitti.

Then, they agree to meet again at a certain intersection in Rome. But for five and a half minutes, late on a sunny evening, the camera notes or admits their absence as life goes on. Duration wipes away plot. The trilogy is often said to be novelistic, and there's truth in that, but these moments of not meeting could hardly be described in literature without seeming ominous or part of a thriller format—and that suggestion was not ruled out in *L'Avventura*. But on the screen, you can see nothing happening without any need to stress it, and it changes not just the mood of a film, but its philosophy.

"… for five and a half minutes, late on a sunny evening, the camera notes or admits their absence as life goes on. Duration wipes away plot."

As life goes on at that intersection so many different contexts are evoked. One is the city itself: a random, interminable series of events, unimportant but factual, not organized but expressive of human gathering in a mute, helpless way—it is surveillance, we would say now, and surveillance nags at us about our lack of meaning. Another is architecture—for we see a building under construction. We also note the helpless unkindness of time, its lack of charity, its indifference to hope. We like to think we are in charge of our time. That's what a meeting presumes. But time does not stop for us. It runs on like a stream, and we are mere bubbles. Above all, the edging toward an anonymous documentary-like form, but one without purpose, begins to let us realize how lovers only see themselves. It is how they try to negotiate life—with a great but fragile excitement. The absence of lovers is other people's life. It carries on.

The abiding question with Antonioni altogether—and it hangs over *The Passenger* (see page 230), too—is whether this is to be regarded with dismay or acceptance. The ending of *L'Eclisse* has not, yet, been too influential. But it stresses how far Antonioni is one of the directors most aware of how film's recording function alters our relationship with life. Were we really there?

PIERROT LE FOU

1965, JEAN-LUC GODARD

A Corpse in the Next Room

Ferdinand (Jean-Paul Belmondo) has a wife and a daughter in Paris, a good job and a swell apartment. Sitting in his bath, he reads to the child about Velazquez, and then he has to go to a ridiculous party where most of the guests are lost in the language and poses of advertising. His life is as good and as bad as that. He wants out and he has two inducements: a chance meeting with the film director Samuel Fuller at the party who tells him cinema is love, hate, action, violence, death—in a word: emotion. The other trigger is the fact that the baby-sitter that night is Marianne (Anna Karina), an old flame. So when Ferdinand drives her home, he keeps going with her. They stay one night at a flat where there happens to be a corpse in the next room while they're making love. Then they head for the South and the summer, "like spirits through a mirror." She calls him Pierrot.

Ferdinand and Marianne on their island retreat.

The director Jean-Luc Godard and the actress Anna Karina had divorced before they made *Pierrot le Fou*, so there was a premeditated anguish to the film that accompanied the summer hues and the red of blood in Raoul Coutard's photography and the halting plaintiveness of Antoine Duhamel's music. It is a film about the end of a love affair, and in hindsight you have to wonder why either Godard or Karina agreed to make it. Unless they both believed that their union was the most tragic thing that had ever happened to them.

So they reach the coast and they live like castaways with a fox and a parrot, a little food and many books. Ferdinand is reading and writing all the time,

and Marianne tells him "You talk to me with words and I look at you with feelings." What past is she looking at?

This clash of intellect and instinct has been filmed many times before—it is the meeting of the professor and Lola in *The Blue Angel*, and it is not too far from Humbert and another Lo in *Lolita*. It is *Middlemarch* and *Ulysses*. But Godard seems to see it as the inevitable barrier between a director and an actress. Of course, they

ABOVE: *Blue and red.*

BELOW: *Red and blue.*

must come together in a burst of creation. And so they made a handful of films, like diamonds lost in the snow. But how could that rapture be sustained?

They talk about the things in life they love. Marianne lists flowers, animals, the blue of the sky, music, and Ferdinand responds with ambition, hope, the movement of things, accidents. You could write a book about the honesty, the lies and the overlap in those lists. Maybe most books come down to it in the end.

But Marianne reacts by saying it's hopeless—"We will never understand each other,"—and she begins a lament, "I don't know what to do."

Before this there has been the supreme, incriminating moment. Ferdinand asks her, "You'll never leave me?" "No, of course not," she replies. "Of course, not?" he pushes her. At which Marianne, sunburned and sullen in close-up, looks straight into the camera, at Godard and us. She says, "Yes, of course," and again, "Yes, of course." You almost want the image to catch fire in the projector, like the sled in the furnace.

Of course, Godard went on, but you can propose that he soon lost the habit of or his faith in simple, pitiless love stories. He had done those, and he had had his old-fashioned movie passion just as he had loved American pictures—like Sam Fuller's and Nick Ray's—in his chilly way. It is still the saddest film I know, and one I fear anew every time I see it. This may start to explain why the intersection at the end of *L'Eclisse* (see page 176) is empty.

"It is a
film about
the end
of a love
affair . . ."

*Jean-Paul Belmondo
and Anna Karina.*

" "We will never understand each other. . ." "

MICKEY ONE

1965, ARTHUR PENN

Anxiety and the City

This is a real film—you can look it up. Written by Alan Surgal and directed by Arthur Penn; it stars Warren Beatty and it has an improvised jazz score by Eddie Sauter that includes Stan Getz on his tenor saxophone. I would not be surprised if you'd never heard of it, and if you saw it you might be as bewildered and displeased as Beatty seems to have been. Even so, two years later, Penn and Beatty collaborated again on *Bonnie and Clyde*.

Beatty plays a brash nightclub comedian in Detroit—he does a stand-up act—until one night he gets carried away in a fling with a gangster's girl. Whereupon the word goes out that he is very bad news, so he does what he can to go under cover and he flees to Chicago, where for a while he lives like

Warren Beatty as Mickey One doing his nightclub act.

a bum. The film is full of broken faces on the street, the kind of faces you see less in motion pictures than in documentary photographs from the Depression or wanted posters—the wanted and the unwanted. The film is shot in harsh black and white by a French cinematographer, Ghislain Cloquet (he also shot Resnais's *Night and Fog* and Bresson's *Mouchette*).

But Mickey is restless and ambitious and he wonders if he might make a comeback in another city, only to feel that old paranoia building up all the time. He gets a post at the Xanadu club, which is run by Hurd Hatfield, as ever beautiful but strange. He finds himself a girl (Alexandra Stewart). We see his act—he's funny in a brash way and he plays piano (just as Beatty did). But he's uneasy. Everyone who saw the film— just a few—said this is a crazy pretentious, French-like film about anxiety and the city, and some people said warily that it was "interesting."

I like it a lot and I cherish this moment. Mickey believes that a nightclub owner in Detroit, Ruby Lapp, may have the answer to his predicament and may know whom he has to pay off, and how much. So he goes to find Lapp—I

OPPOSITE: *Trying to hide, Mickey becomes a bum in Chicago.*

"… the kind of faces you see less in motion pictures than in documentary photographs from the Depression or wanted posters …"

Ruby Lapp (Franchot Tone) knows the answers. He even knows the questions.

feel pretty sure in a paranoid kind of way that the name of the character was meant to make us think of Jack Ruby. You were likely thinking of him still in 1965, anyway.

Lapp is played by Franchot Tone, who was then sixty, though he looked much older. Tone, born to great wealth, had been an actor with the Group

Theatre, and he made a lot of movies and had a very muddled romantic career: He was married to four actresses—Joan Crawford, Jean Wallace, Barbara Payton and Dolores Dorn. That may explain why he looked much older than sixty. He would be dead in three years, and this was his swan song. So Mickey comes to him and he says, maybe it's as much as $20,000 he owes to the Mob. At that point, Lapp gives out with this great speech:

"How do you know it's $20,000? I didn't say $20,000. How do you know it's only money? Or all the other crap games they tore up on you, and the bookie slips? How do you know it's not the car they gave you you smashed up? Or the liquor, and the good times and the parties and the clothes, and Christmas and birthdays and the rehearsal hall? How do you know it isn't the trips they paid for, the special material, the arrangements in music? The dentist, the lawsuits, the parties? The expenses! Twenty thousand dollars? Twenty thousand dollars is just a fraction. How do you know it isn't your whole life you are living?"

Tone does not ham it up, but he makes it sound like one of the grave closing-out speeches in Chekhov, or something Uncle Jack might have told George in *The Magnificent Ambersons*. It's a speech that seems luminous now, as if someone felt compelled to capture the dread of the sixties—with the assassinations and the intrigues and the loss of confidence in government or the country as a whole. It could come off as a literary speech, and you may think of it that way still, but Franchot Tone gives it a vitality and a foreboding, a fatalistic humor, as if he surely knew this was the moment of his career.

"Tone does not ham it up, but he makes it sound like one of the grave closing-out speeches in Chekhov . . ."

BLOW-UP

1966, MICHELANGELO ANTONIONI

Plots Real and Imagined

Thomas (David Hemmings) is a photographer in an age that had made a fetish out of photographs. It was the 1960s in London and he knew that he could do astonishingly erotic fashion shots and pictures of social rejects in flophouses from one minute to the next. The Sunday magazines would put them side by side and think themselves daring. Like fixative, the same glamour washed over them both, and he was cool and cute for taking the two types of picture without being concerned or involved.

He's not much more than a boy, but he likely makes a fortune. He has a car, a studio and his own place and he has his own time. He has groupies who will show him everything if he'll take their picture. Wherever he finds himself, he is likely to have a camera. It is his best companion.

One summer day he goes to a pleasant suburban park. There are not many people around but he sees a couple, an attractive woman (Vanessa Redgrave) and a rather older man (Ronan O'Casey). Are they lovers, or are they quarreling? He takes pictures of them—it is his only way of finding out or relating to the world. He shoots off a roll but the woman notices him and she is alarmed. Has she lost her privacy or her soul? She comes up to him and demands the film. He is insolent; he resists her. Later on she will try in her awkward way to trade her body for the roll of film. He fools her. And now comes the moment.

There is an extended scene, without talk, in which he develops and prints his shots. Sometimes he makes enlargements. As he works he begins to wonder if there is a story or a meaning in the series of pictures. He is led to believe

"Are they lovers, or are they quarreling?"

that he may have seen something like a murder. For there is what looks like a body, and there is even what could be the figure of an assassin in the bushes. People looked very closely at photographs and grassy knolls in the 60s, and surely they saw things in them. I think in the history of photography it was a critical moment. Today, we are far more bored with pictures. We do not believe our fate hinges on them. We know not to trust them.

It is a Michelangelo Antonioni film, shot in English and in England, and it was a moderate international hit because of the way it seemed to identify swinging London—though that had a lot to do with the pulse of photography. It came from a story by Julio Cortázar and Antonioni did a script with Tonino Guerra for which the playwright Edward Bond wrote English dialogue. I'm

Vanessa Redgrave as the woman from the park, doing what it takes to get the pictures back.

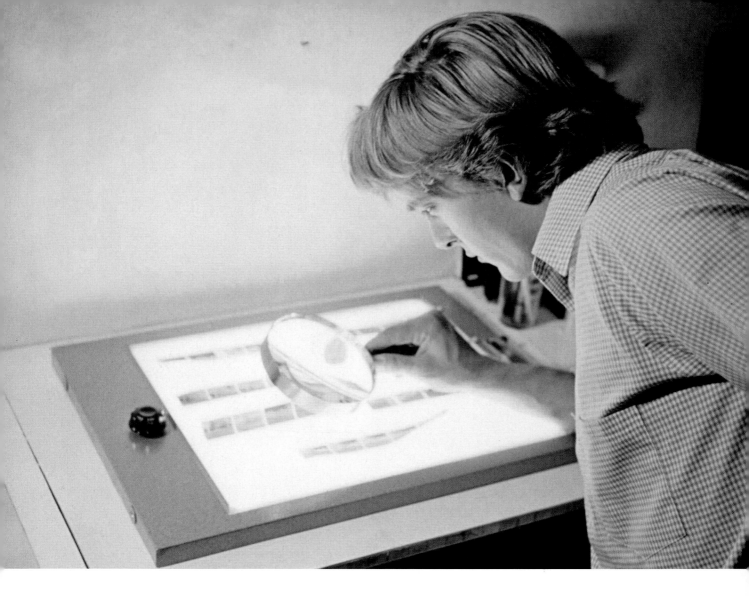

" ... he may have seen something like a murder."

sure that I was not the only film teacher who used this sequence as an impetus to get students to think in storyboards, in lines of images. But Antonioni's breathless moment—with just the rustle of the trees in the park and the click of a camera (or is it an automatic weapon?)—was asking, are we helpless fools who see a plot or a story everywhere? It was a great age of plots, both real and imagined, and I'm not sure that movie suspense ever meant quite the same after we lost that sense of pictures as fetishes of reality.

Blow-Up never answers its own mystery. Thomas's pictures are stolen; he has nowhere to go with his "story." I suppose he becomes more detached than ever. He seems to have become a puppet whose strings have been tied. That was another sign of the times. So many films would have refused to abandon the thriller element. Everything would have had to be explained (think of the resolution to Coppola's *The Conversation*, which is a blow-up of sound). But Antonioni was one of those who guessed that, despite being

190

the truth twenty-four times a second (that's what Jean-Luc Godard said, but it was less insight than a photo of insight), film posed better questions than answers. After all, most of the great intrigues of the 60s—the real ones, with grassy knolls—have remained unsolved. But all these years later, as you watch Thomas's images come to life, you wish you could look again in that very young, credulous way.

"... Antonioni was one of those who guessed that ... film posed better questions than answers."

POINT BLANK

1967, JOHN BOORMAN

Magisterial Cool

Walker (Lee Marvin) was an ordinary enough roughneck with a bit of the outlaw in his soul. He had a wife he loved, Lynne (Sharon Acker), and a best buddy, Mal Reese (John Vernon), and the three of them planned to steal some money on the Alcatraz run. Some other thieves went to Alcatraz Island in the San Francisco Bay after a job to split their money. That's where Walker and Reese would jump them and take the loot. But Reese shot Walker, left him for dead, and went off with the money and Lynne.

What are you going to believe when you see the badly wounded Walker staggering into the water off Alcatraz and hoping to make the very testing swim back to the mainland? It is Lee Marvin, isn't it? So Walker resurrects himself and he starts off in pursuit of his $93,000. He doesn't want the earth, but he's stubborn, and he's Lee Marvin, and he doesn't care who stands in his way. So he climbs the staircase of the criminal organization, eliminating unpleasant men at every step, and along the way he's observed and aided by Yost (Keenan Wynn), the bleak accountant. Walker enlists Lynne's sister, Chris, after the remorseful Lynne has killed herself, and he uses Chris as bait—this is Angie Dickinson in and out of a yellow dress—to get to Mal Reese and that's the end of Reese. But he still wants the $93,000.

And finally, Yost tells him, very well, he can have his stupid money. They'll do the transaction back in San Francisco, but not at Alcatraz. They'll do it in the old fort at Fort Point, from which you can see Alcatraz. It's a large building with a courtyard and several floors of galleries. Walker is there at night and he is hiding in the shadows. A helicopter brings in the package, Yost has his assassin (James Sikking) kill off the last of his rivals, Brewster (Carroll O'Connor), and he calls out to Walker to come down and get the money. It's business. Nothing happens.

This is the end of John Boorman's film (one of those unexpected visions of America made by a stranger, an Englishman), from a novel by Donald Westlake, scripted by Alexander Jacobs. What are you going to believe? Is Walker smart enough to realize that he can't trust anyone? Does he guess that as soon as he appears in the light in the courtyard, some marksman is going to pick him off so that Yost can save the money and have nothing else to fear?

If a man like Yost understands a life without fear. Does Walker elect to merge with the darkness? Will he retire and take Chris off to a peaceful, secluded life in somewhere like Hana on Maui, maybe? As if they couldn't find you in Hana if they wanted to. Might be their first guess.

Or has Walker been dead all the time? Why not assume that when Mal Reese shot a dangerous rival he knew what he was doing and did it for keeps. In which case, is the whole story of "Where is my $93,000?" the dream of a dying man in which he proves to himself that he is superb, unkillable and capable of toppling the Organization? Does he think he's Lee Marvin?

There are plenty of other moments in *Point Blank* to treasure—like the sequence where a frustrated Chris turns on every electrical appliance in the house to disturb Walker's magisterial cool. But nothing is as arresting or as hard to shake as the courtyard at Fort Point when everyone has gone away, and a parcel of money is left on the ground, knocked open to reveal that it is real money and not just white paper bills. Who cares—it's only $93,000. Then the camera lifts up and looks out over the bay at night and we see the blinking light on Alcatraz. Some San Franciscans will always love *Vertigo* and its part in city mythology, but I opt for the mystery of *Point Blank* and people who will not die defeated.

When Walker finds his wife is dead, he moves on to her sister. Lee Marvin and Angie Dickinson.

*What a man will do
for $93,000. Especially
if he's dead already.*

"Does
Walker elect
to merge
with the
darkness?"

BONNIE AND CLYDE

1967, ARTHUR PENN

Seductive Little Scene

You know very well that you think I'm going to pick the big shoot-'em-up at the end, where B & C are shot to pieces, in slow motion, and the way they roll and loll and twitch is like the great orgasm that has always been coming for them without ever quite arriving. But you've heard and seen that analyzed so many times you could do the moment yourself. You know it! Don't tell me you don't do moments as you're waiting to go to sleep. So I'm going back to calmer and happier days, to a quite seductive little scene.

Very soon after these adorable hoodlums have met, with Clyde (Warren Beatty) looking up and Bonnie (Faye Dunaway) naked at the upstairs window, you know this is a love story. So Clyde pitches woo the only way he knows how: He holds up a grocery store out in the west Texas countryside and Bonnie is so impressed she's ready to have him right there in the getaway car. But Clyde holds back: "I ain't much of a lover boy. . . . I never saw no percentage in it." And Bonnie is flat-out taken aback: "Your advertising is just dandy. Folks'd never guess you don't have a thing to sell."

This is a very intriguing moment in what was Beatty's first foray into production—he was the one who had snapped up the Robert Benton–David Newman script when they were trying to get Truffaut or Godard to do it. And Beatty, as you may recall, had a famous reputation as a ladies' man, though a few years later in *Shampoo* he played a character who got all the more women by letting the feeling get around among other men that, as a hairdresser, he might be gay.

So there was a way in which both Clyde and Beatty needed to reassert themselves, and that's my moment. Instead of taking her home, as she asks, Clyde takes Bonnie to a small, scruffy café. He sits her down in a booth and he starts to educate her in what a producer does. First of all, he tells this raving beauty what a lousy no-account life she's living in Texas. He guesses that when she was sixteen or seventeen, some idiot took advantage of her who worked in a . . . ? And Bonnie fills in the gap with, "a ce-ment factory," and the stress on that word let you know there and then this was going to be a film you could eat like ice cream. It was serving itself up. Why? It was produced!

"... when ... and how ... am I ever ... gonna get away from this?"

196

He lays it on her the trap she's in: about the guys who "ask you for dates and sometimes you go . . . but you mostly don't, because all they ever try to do is get in your pants whether you want 'em or not . . . So you go on home and you sit in your room and you think, now when . . . and how . . . am I ever . . . gonna get away from this?" He has her. He pauses and then he says, "And now you know."

Sometimes talking to a woman and letting her know you know her can leave coition itself, or whatever it's called, a formality. But then Clyde applies the coup de grace. Just like the waitress in the café, Bonnie is wearing a stupid spit curl. He points at her hair and says, "Change that. I don't like it." She obeys and it is a big improvement. "Shiiit," he sighs. "You're a knockout." His knockout.

Soon enough they're on the road, picking up C. W. Moss and Buck Barrow and Blanche, and the murderous chase is on. And just as Clyde has made this far-fetched Bonnie into a movie star fit for Faye and fit for Warren, so near the end Bonnie will write a ballad "poem" about them which gets in the papers. It's payback: "You told my story!" Clyde enthuses. It's a film about Warren and Faye making it, which in Hollywood is rather more important than making out, or whatever it's called.

"And now you know."

THE CONFORMIST

1970, BERNARDO BERTOLUCCI

The Pain, The Damage, the Evil and the Horror

For much of the time in *The Conformist*, Clerici (Jean-Louis Trintignant) is getting ready for a fateful car journey with Manganiello (Gastone Moschin). In other words, he knows where he is going; he is conforming to a plan and a character type he has chosen for himself. One of the things that makes *The Conformist* such a striking examination of the fascist personality is the way Clerici has abandoned human nature to be an actor playing himself. So everything in his life is calculated, apart from those few tragic mistakes he makes—like murdering the chauffeur who seduced him as a child and falling in something like real love with Anna Quadri (Dominique Sanda), the young wife of the liberal professor he has vowed to assassinate.

Trintignant and Dominique Sanda in love and betrayal. His hat is like an attitude.

So we see his two deranged parents as people this assigned personality can disregard; we see his frivolous but beautiful wife (Stefania Sandrelli) as a sex toy he revels in as if she was a prize whore. We see him at confession when his chief aim is to outrage the priest. And all the time we observe the magnificent hunched, enclosed walk Trintignant has devised for Clerici, as if it was his dominant ambition to go unnoticed. Because he does not want to see himself. That is the trick to being a fascist, and believing you are doing it for a necessary script.

But the men who made this picture—director Bernardo Bertolucci, photographer Vittorio Storaro, designer Ferdinando Scarfiotti, and the composer Georges Delerue—have conspired in one of film's outstanding, though controlled, displays of beauty. This is not picturesque, self-indulgent or spectacular; rather it is a remarkable occasion for the cohesive expressiveness of all the elements in filmmaking. But it is exactly that richness that most offends or

OPPOSITE:
The Conformist is a confrontation between human reality and classical ideals; Jean-Louis Trintignant as the assassin.

201

"He is conforming to a character he has chosen for himself."

conflicts Clerici, for it keeps stressing that the world and its moments are breathtaking, where he wants them to be the organized stages of a pageant or a parade.

So the journey, the car ride, meets its destiny, a gloomily dark forest with a winding road. This is where the killers are waiting, where the cars stop and Quadri is butchered. But Anna, in ivory white, runs back to the lurking, parked car and finds Clerici sitting like a toad in its darkness. She had guessed his nature, but she had been seduced by him anyway. Fascism can have an erotic allure. But now she realizes the full wickedness, and her own destruction. She screams and runs away but the anonymous killers—in hats and coats like shrouds—will track her down, and Clerici is fulfilled.

There are so many killings in movies, and so many of them don't bother with the pain, the damage, the evil and the horror, or even notice such things. In *The Conformist*, nothing is omitted and Clerici is left as one of the most hateful yet warning figures in the movies.

OPPOSITE: *One of the most hideous murders in film history: the professor in the forest.*

She sees him watching and beats on the window. But we are watching, too.

203

KLUTE

1971, ALAN J. PAKULA

Sex, Lies, and Videotape

John Klute (Donald Sutherland) is a policeman in a small town in Pennsylvania who quits the force to search for a scientist who has disappeared. Sutherland could be very sharp and knowing (as in *MASH* or *Don't Look Now*), or he could be hollow-eyed and nearly vacant, as in *The Day of the Locust* or *Klute*. Why does the film have my name? he seems to wonder. It's a good question since the picture quickly becomes a study of Bree Daniels, a sometime actress and occasional hooker, whose name was found in the missing man's diary. So Klute goes out of his element, to New York City, to try to keep up with the fast mind and rough tongue of Bree (Jane Fonda).

As written by Andy and Dave Lewis, directed by Alan J. Pakula and shot by Gordon Willis (just before he did *The Godfather*), *Klute* is one of the most suggestive paranoid films of the 70s and a study of female performance and self-awareness that may have been influenced by the Godard films of a few years earlier (*Vivre Sa Vie*, *Une Femme Mariée*, *Masculine Feminine*).

Fonda had already allowed herself to be the subject of one of the cinema-verité documentaries made by Robert Drew and Richard Leacock. In *Klute* we see at least four levels of her "act": auditioning for roles; the professional life of a prostitute; talking to her analyst about her life; and being the Bree who realizes how much under threat she is and who begins to fall in love with Klute, even if he hardly seems the soundest guy in the world.

For he watches her: It is a film about recording, wiretapping, surveillance and voyeurism, and the moment I treasure is seen silent through the watchful gaze of Klute from the rooftop of another building as Bree services one of her clients. He is an old and wealthy man and all she has to do is visit him at night and begin to disrobe. There is no actual sex, though we may be reminded that for decades any hint at undressing was about the most erotic thing the movies could offer. It is a scene of melancholy gentleness, filled with the limits of old age—just as it is a moment in which Bree can exult in her authority. In fact, she looks like a great movie actress in the scene (and Fonda won the Oscar as Bree), but she tells her shrink that whoring makes up for her failures as an actress because it gives her a brief sense of power and control.

"...a study of female performance and self-awareness..."

204

"... it is a film about recording, wiretapping, surveillance and voyeurism ..."

Pakula would become fascinated with paranoia and he was deeply interested in psychiatry. Gordon Willis makes so much of this picture a study in the colors of night and stealth, while there is a moaning, sighing score by Michael Small that often gives the sense of some spying figure breathing and being aroused. But this film was Fonda's moment, just as it was rapt with feelings of sexual danger. She is tough but vulnerable, desperate to hold on to some truth in the stormy ways Bree keeps trying to rate herself. With the old man, she has a moment of peace and ease. She is queen of the night's harem. (The question left hanging is, Can she have sex or love with John Klute?)

OPPOSITE AND BELOW: *Klute is a counterculture movie in which Bree (Jane Fonda) is always teasing her john (Donald Sutherland).*

THE KING OF MARVIN GARDENS

1972, BOB RAFELSON

Telling a Story

As I compose this book, I am beginning to realize that many of my moments turn on story—the way it is told, or not told—and I wonder if the entire history of film, or movie, doesn't have a lot to do with the way human culture sought to abandon or lose believable stories; in other words, film has served as a transition between the novel and . . . well, whatever will come next.

David Staebler is telling a story. It is just his face, half-lit in the dark, and he is Jack Nicholson, and at this time in our lives Nicholson, or Jack, was starting to be some kind of touchstone of reliability or American soundness. He is telling a story about his childhood with his brother Jason and their grandfather, about the night the old man got a fish bone stuck in his throat and choked to death. "Don't ever tell anyone about this," Jason orders David in the story. Yet David is telling the story. Is he talking to himself, or to us? Do we have any place or legitimacy in a film, or is it all an act to fool us? It's harder to think that if only because David and Jack tell this story with such feeling. You can see it happening. You can feel the loss in the boys' lives, you can feel the death of the older man and how it led to a pact between the brothers. Because, you see, in the story, as the old man is choking the boys do nothing—they don't even give him a flat heel of pumpernickel to clear his throat.

Then a dull red light flashes on David's face. It's the control room. He's on the radio, late-night radio, telling the story. He has a show. He goes home and there is the grandfather, a wreck of a survivor, who must have heard the show, because he coughs in mockery of David's lies. If a story is ever as clear-cut as a lie.

This is *The King of Marvin Gardens*, the film Nicholson and director Bob Rafelson made after *Five Easy Pieces*—that one has the much better known moment of Jack in the diner ordering an omelet with a side of toast. But I prefer *The King of Marvin Gardens*—which is not a widely shared taste.

The movie turns out to be a story about the two brothers (Bruce Dern plays Jason), and in their different ways they are both storytellers. David is a solitary and a depressive, without too much of a life, and he yarns away into the microphone as if those lies were harmless. But Jason is a real-life dreamer and schemer who has huge plans to transform their lives, and those stories are

"Is he talking to himself, or to us?"

David and Jason Staebler—the bipolar condition in one family (Jack Nicholson and Bruce Dern).

209

dangerous, even if Jason is the life and soul of the party, trying to balance two women (Ellen Burstyn and Julia Anne Robinson).

I love the radio story sequence, the radio story, because it's one of those moments where Jack allowed his bonhomie to be stripped away and let us see the inward fellow he may be. And although movies had always played to crowds in their great days—packed houses—I think there's a way in which their

"…it's one of those moments where Jack… let us see the inward fellow he may be."

entrance to fantasy and their encouragement to tell our quiet stories was always playing to loneliness. Again, that could be relevant to what happened to story. Once upon a time, story was a gathering force, but nowadays it's easier and sadder to see that story is a mark of privacy and solitude. Of course, in 1972 *The King of Marvin Gardens* didn't do well, but today I suspect it would do much better because so many of us have arrived at its darkness.

THE GODFATHER

1972, FRANCIS FORD COPPOLA

The Right Calm

I think everyone knows and loves this scene as much as they like Italian food, a nice glass of Chianti, and those quiet, neighborhood restaurants, unboasting classics, where made men can go for a serious conversation. Michael Corleone (Al Pacino) has stepped forward with the attempted murder of his father. He has turned up at the hospital at the providential moment, with just the timid baker Enzo (Gabriele Torrei) as help, and he has noticed that his hand doesn't shake when he lights a cigarette. He isn't afraid of the challenge; he has the right calm in his blood. (There's a moment in *20,000 Years in Sing Sing*, from 1933, where Spencer Tracy seeks a light for a last cigarette before he goes to the chair. Then he has to hold the good-natured Warden's match steady. These things are in the family of film.)

So Michael makes his meeting with Sollozzo (Al Lettieri) and McCluskey (Sterling Hayden), the crooked cop. They frisk him in their car, of course, but the revolver, its butt wrapped in duct tape, will be behind the lavatory cistern in the men's room of a restaurant. All Michael has to do is ask to be excused. Come out with the gun in his hand, shoot the two men at the table. Drop the gun and walk away as if he's finished his meal. When Michael outlines the plan to the others—Sonny, Tessio, Clemenza, Tom Hagen—they step back in awe and amusement. It is not quite clear yet that Michael has taken over, much less what he will become.

There is small talk at the restaurant. "Try the veal," urges Sollozzo. There is talk in Italian. It is a pretty but ordinary place, ironed white tablecloths, a long and narrow shape, with only a few other customers (as designed and dressed by Dean Tavoularis). Cinematographer Gordon Willis has given it a nice walnut gloom. There's only one thing wrong (if you think about it—and you don't at first): You can hear the subway trains passing, which is not what an intimate neighborhood place makes its reputation on. But the post-production sound designer Walter Murch knows that if there's music on the track then sound is theater, and the roar of the train will be an extra source of suspense and crisis.

Michael goes to the men's room—the conjunction of eating and waste is not by chance, I think—and finds the gun. The train noise builds and he comes out, sits again for a moment and then he stands and executes them. Sollozzo falls back. McCluskey is shot in the act of eating, in the throat and the head, with a white napkin tucked into the neckband of his uniform. Then he tumbles forward into his own pasta.

The music soars in romantic triumph (it is by Nino Rota, and it would fit a fateful love scene), and Michael departs, though he only remembers to

"We want these bastards dead."

drop the gun at the last instant. It seems to feel like shit on his hands. A black car is waiting for him outside. The world has changed.

His father, Vito (Marlon Brando), knows only a little about this—he is an invalid after his shooting. But he is filled with regret. He would not want Michael involved. This was the Ivy League son, the military hero he hoped to keep out of the business and the shit. But the scene is constructed and shot like a coming of age. A trial by arms. An initiation. Which means that we are on the side of the murderous enterprise. We want these bastards dead. We want clean shots and an epic aftermath, the tableau of the ruined table. It is a legend in the moment of its making, a story to be told and re-enacted down the ages. It is like a pledge of allegiance for a country that cher-

"It's not me, Kay— it's my family."

ishes big shoot-outs. So it's not just Michael who has been enlisted in the family and its code of violence. It is us, too. And there is a long way to go before director Francis Coppola poses the test of whether or not Michael is fit company, or whether his lethal calm has embraced us and corrupted us.

"His father . . . would not want Michael involved. This was the Ivy League son, the military hero . . ."

PAT GARRETT & BILLY THE KID

1973, SAM PECKINPAH

Too Many Moments

All too often, there are great moments in movies that have to go—because there are just too many moments. So it was years before this scene from *Pat Garrett & Billy the Kid* was ever delivered to the public. But it's a scene that permits a gentle alteration in the entire tone of a great film. It is also the kind of material that the director, Sam Peckinpah, was not famous for thinking of, let alone filming. But the scene survived and now it is there in some DVDs. There are probably five thousand scenes as intriguing and more fully lost in the collected vaults of the movie business. Sometimes they are the best scenes. After all, artists who have to edit are raised on the pitiless wisdom: Be ready to murder your favorite children.

Garrett is the sheriff of Lincoln County, New Mexico. He has captured his old friend, William Bonney, the Kid, and then the Kid has escaped, killing two deputies in the process. So Garrett is affronted and even humiliated, and he is still hired to eliminate an old friend and someone whose love of wild liberty he once shared. But "times they are a-changin'." Garrett is an official, an instrument of progress—in which neither the Kid nor the film has any faith.

The scene occurs just after the languid, face-saving performance where Garrett visits the barber shop. He has a dandy in him as well as a womanizer (later we will see him in bed, contented, with three whores). So he repairs his

image, and hires Alamosa Bill (Jack Elam) as a reluctant deputy. He is putting his world back in order. He is smooth, suave and perfumed—he may have that sweet air about him that makes Wyatt Earp (Henry Fonda) wince in *My Darling Clementine*.

In the movie as first released. Garrett is next seen out on the range, looking for the Kid. But that lost another scene in town where the sheriff walks back to his house, his home. He is a property owner, where Billy is a nomadic creature. It is a small, tidy, pretty white house with a garden, a white fence and a wife.

She is Mexican (played by Aurora Clavel). She is neither young nor glamorous but she is discontented. She is also based on history. It was in 1880 (the period of the film) that Garrett married Apolinaria Gutierrez, the sister of his first wife, who had died. Patrick Garrett and Apolinaria had nine children.

In the film, the wife is not named and children are not seen, but as soon as the scene begins she attacks Garrett for the problems he presents as a husband—missing meals, not being kind or honorable. This is not the kind of convenient whore a roaming Westerner may pick up on his travels. This is a commitment in which the husband is failing and for which he has no adequate or decent answer beyond storming out of the house. Let me add that "difficult" women in Peckinpah are sometimes hit, shot or raped. They are seldom listened to.

Is that why the scene was dropped? Did it rub against Peckinpah's grain when he saw it? I think it's more likely that studio people complained that the scene didn't go anywhere—it was an aside. The wife does not reappear. There is always a tendency in filmmaking to cut those uneventful moments that do not add up. But sometimes they carry the impressions that last longest.

As Garrett goes out on the trail, he camps beside a river and in the evening a family floats by on a raft. It is their mobile home, so much less stable and progressive than Garrett's house. The man on the raft is shooting at drifting targets. Garrett competes in a free, playful spirit. But the raft man is hostile. He points his rifle at Garrett on the shore. There is a standoff, and then it passes. It is a scene that could be dropped. But it is a moment of beauty that captures the last days of the unfettered life of the West before family, community, law, order, shopping malls and antidepressants set in.

While hunting for the Kid, Garrett (James Coburn) rests up with three spectacular whores—better than New Mexico offered in 1881? Well, Billy the Kid didn't look like Kris Kristofferson, either.

"There are probably five thousand scenes as intriguing . . . lost in the collected vaults of the movie business."

DON'T LOOK NOW

1973, NICOLAS ROEG

Alone Together

In Venice, in winter, wearing brown in the misty white light, John and Laura Baxter return to their hotel. They are a married couple; this is a film about marriage in that married people have such access to their own sexuality that perhaps they no longer take zealous advantage of it. A thing called normal life has intruded on their concentration. Entirely together, married people may drift apart; they begin to notice differences where once they were riveted by the way they rhymed with each other.

This marriage is recovering from the loss by drowning of one of their children—in an English pond, on another misty day. They have gone to Venice because he is an art historian who has a job there on church restoration. But even in winter the trip is a merciful vacation, too, so they are tender to each other, watchful and sympathetic. There is no hint that this marriage has ever been in trouble; there is every suggestion that the shared loss may begin to make them lovers again.

John and Laura are also Donald Sutherland and Julie Christie, and we do not need to have it explained that they were fond at the time. There is something casual yet intimate in the ways they touch and look at each other that goes beyond acting—indeed, it might look studied or even sinister if actors began to put this naturalism into professional practice. And although *Don't Look Now* is a thriller, a mystery, or even a horror picture, still here comes an interlude (or a deepening) that feels like a concession to their marriage. We do not know whether it is the first time they have made love since the loss of their daughter. But there is a sense of recovery or forgiveness, and it depends on the moment having no immediate bearing on the plot.

John and Laura go up to their hotel suite, an expensive affair, in the brown-and-white motif we have seen in the winter light, and which will be borne out in this use of nakedness, hair, nipples and mouths. She takes a bath; he has a shower. This is 1973, with brave, "naked" acting, and the players let us see breasts, hair and private parts without a trace of coyness. They seem to be alone together. And only slowly, silently, does lovemaking arise as an idea. He is naked, she is in a robe. They are lying on their bed together. Looking at a newspaper. She has remarked on toothpaste left on his mouth and he has

OPPOSITE ABOVE:
In filming love scenes, it's hard to escape the presence of actors pretending. Donald Sutherland and Julie Christie.

OPPOSITE BELOW: *In the 60s and 70s, nakedness became a motif or a genre in movies—but usually with actresses.*

218

invited her to eat it off. But that was a while ago, and all that happens is that her absentminded hand goes to his back and his bottom to stroke them, to touch someone, as if in the dark, to know he is there?

They begin to make love, and by 1973 there was a feeling in cinema that the time had come for that thing to be seen and felt. But then, in a loving but intrusive gesture, as he parts the flaps of her robe, the better to kiss or taste her, the movie cuts to another parting, as John slides hangers on a wardrobe rack, searching for what he will wear afterward, when they go out to dinner.

That is the structure of the sequence (directed by Nicolas Roeg and edited by Graeme Clifford). It is a beautifully composed sequence, and yet the scheme (of showing the lovemaking next to the reconstruction of polite appearance perhaps thirty minutes later) is more than an editor would offer. The plan is a part of the film's direction, even if there is no such passage in the Daphne du Maurier short story.

The crosscutting does nothing to diminish or restrict the passion; nor is it there out of squeamishness or to skirt censorship. Yet cutting away from sex on the screen has served both those drab purposes in its time. The rising enjoyment of these two is erotic and open, no matter that their bodies are not *Playboy*ish and the light never seeks that amber glow the movies have stupidly inherited from pinup photography. Instead, the small flashes forward are witty: The pants coming up over Laura's black panties are a nice joke about composure once we have seen her pubic hair. When she puts mascara on the eyes and buttons up the pearl-gray cardigan, the primness is comic after the lunging of their bodies. And the wistful smile on Christie's face when she considers her own lipstick is part of the joy that can contemplate love retrospectively. How wild we were once!

These moments are only half an hour apart, but the adjacency on screen is a commentary on time and eternity. These could be old people remembering their youth. They could be separated by divorce, or even death. And while I don't intend to spoil the story in *Don't Look Now*, things won't work out well for the Baxters. So the lovemaking has been turned into a lifelong reverie. It helps that the scene is so silent. These lovers say nothing; they do not sigh or moan. Their open mouths are cut off from sound's immediacy just as abandon is folded into dressing and getting ready.

The poetry in all cutting serves to divide and marry, and that is the ultimate insight: In the most rapturous union, these are separate people, different minds though the bodies cling together and slide in and out of each other.

Whenever movies flash backward or forward to survey our whole life the results tend to be bromide clichés (the actors picking up flour in their hair). But this gap of thirty minutes has opened up a feeling for time that is novelistic, or something the power of cutting in movies has neglected. I love this

"**They could be separated by divorce, or even death.**"

moment in *Don't Look Now*—for Roeg's boldness, for the valor of the actors, and for the tender sense of marriage—but those very qualities set up the disappointment of *Don't Look Now*. The depth of insight for five minutes or so only underlines how far the rest of the film settles for melodrama and a strained notion of the occult.

That's opinion, of course. There are viewers who find *Don't Look Now* a satisfying thriller. For me, the grisly conclusion is mere cruelty after the compassion of this married moment. That contrast points up the gap between promise and fulfillment in Roeg's career. He began as a cameraman and there are critics who have remarked on how far he seemed to think through the camera (this was curiously supported by his inarticulate interviews).

There are great passages in Roeg—in this, in *Walkabout* and *Bad Timing*, yet whole films feel unattended. Still, in a mosaic of moments, *Don't Look Now* seems essential—for its eroticism, and by the pointer toward a kind of moviemaking that we do not yet enjoy enough, one in which the cinema's appetite for time could mean so much. So as we see the moment again, we feel pain for the Baxters, for Roeg's letdown, and for ourselves and this medium. There are mysteries greater than a red dwarf in the shadows of Venice.

Don't Look Now has a sex scene that involves reconstruction after abandonment. Is it sexier?

221

CELINE AND JULIE GO BOATING

1974, JACQUES RIVETTE

A Movie House

It happens this way: one sleepy summer afternoon in one of those small, hidden squares in Paris, like tarragon in a salad, Julie (Dominique Labourier) is minding her own business, reading—she is a librarian, an apparently decent young woman with her wits and her sense of order intact. Not enough. For all of a sudden, Celine (Juliet Berto) comes by, scattered, colorful, impetuous, dropping things as she goes. She is a cabaret magician, it turns out, or a mad hatter who never bothers to notice the Alice who follows her when she drops something. So they become acquaintances, or friends, on that warm afternoon. Or is this an act they have done before? Do they keep doing it until some arc begins to develop? Don't you sometimes feel that you've done nearly everything before as you wait to be overtaken by a story?

At a very leisurely pace, their friendship builds and they begin to think that something mysterious and interesting is happening at one house—the address is 7 bis rue du Nadir aux Pommes. So far, the director Jacques Rivette has shot this film with elegant unconcern. It's nicely done, tidy, but it looks as natural as the setting, not casual, not "documentary," but very relaxed—it's a way of observing that draws more attention to these oddly assorted women and the way they become attached. It's a matter-of-fact telling of a story that will turn into a seminal examination of fiction.

Celine and Julie gain access to the house, at first singly, then together, and when they emerge, they stagger out of the door as if they had been on a giddy roundabout, at a far-reaching séance, or a rock concert. They compare notes and they realize that something is going on in the house, something that needs their attention. Three adults, two women (Bulle Ogier and Marie-France Pisier) and a man (Barbet Schroeder), are hatching a plot that turns on a little girl, Madeleine. So Celine and Julie go to the house as if it is an ongoing crisis—or a movie house.

You see, the people in the house do not notice our two bold visitors, any more than any film notices *us* in the darkness. And then, gradually, in color, the imagery within the house becomes stylized, like an RKO noir (*Out of the Past?*) and the words and attitudes of the adults in the house become more melodramatic.

"…a story that will turn into a seminal examination of fiction."

The film within the film: Bulle Ogier, Marie-France Pisier and Barbet Schroeder.

" ...something is going on in the house ..."

Juliet Berto and Dominique Labourier watching the show.

There is a moment when Celine and Julie sit together watching this show, and they are just like the man and the city woman in Murnau's *Sunrise* (see page 21), watching the show called "The City" and imagining they might be there one day. The action inside the house seems to play every day, just like a movie, though the women detect small and alarming advances in the story that beg for intervention. I told you this was a leisurely film (it runs three hours and thirteen minutes), but I think it is the most beguiling and adventurous comedy on the whole process of watching movies—and then (Celine is a magician) entering into them and altering their course of action. I am not going to tell you this moment, let alone describe it, because it is the climax of the film and it manages to be exultant, serene, comic and sinister all at the same time. But there is a boat.

This film has not yet been put on DVD in America, and I like it all the more for that. So it is hard to get at, elusive, difficult to see—and its length has always put it in some box-office peril. Still, we should not be deceived by the chronic availability of DVDs. We need to know there are unattainable things, or films we must search for. Or wait for. There is no desire without that frustration. The ability to dial up any movie on our computer or our inner eye may be useful, and it will surely come to pass, but it is one of the things that may drain away the quality of desire in the medium.

OPPOSITE: *Juliet Berto as Celine, the magician.*

CHINATOWN

1974, ROMAN POLANSKI

As Tough as Life

This is a story set in Los Angeles, in 1937, that's just two years before Raymond Chandler published his seminal novel, *The Big Sleep.* You may recall that Philip Marlowe in that book, and Humphrey Bogart in the film (see page 81) were not just superior beings and shabby supermen. They were facing danger and intrigue for next to nothing, because they believed in right, liked to kiss the girl now and then, and hoped to get off a few choice wisecracks. Jake Gittes in *Chinatown*, despite the smiling presence of Jack Nicholson and his cocksure attitude, is not nearly as expert. He gets his nose slit. He tells a crass, dirty joke unaware there's a lady (Faye Dunaway) standing behind him. One way or another, that lady is killed, shot through the eye. The granddaughter goes back to the evil embrace of Noah Cross (John Huston) and not one damn thing is done in Los Angeles to arrest Cross or take away from his authority. So *Chinatown* is shot through with nostalgia for the city that once was and a deep respect for the Marlowe attitude. But neither works, if they ever did. The city has been taken over. It's too big to fail.

BELOW: *"She's my sister…She's my daughter." Faye Dunaway at the end of* Chinatown.

There is a showdown scene where the failure suddenly stares us in the face. Gittes is confronting Noah Cross. He knows how Hollis Mulwray (the water expert) was killed. He has the spectacles he found in the saltwater pond. He can pin it all on Cross. And he can rebuke the man who raped his own daughter so that she gave birth to her sister.

Gittes is waiting in the Mulwray house at dusk as Cross arrives. The old man comes in wearing his Western hat still and he soon realizes how much the private eye knows. Gittes tells him it's murder, and more, and the citizens are going to be "irate"—he's a sentimental liberal. Huston's dreamy voice eases that likelihood away; "That's all taken care of. You see, Mr. Gittes. Either you bring the water to L.A.—or you bring L.A. to the water." This is the voice and the confidence of the pragmatism that made America: It is the ethos of the Western greeting the twentieth century.

The detective is flummoxed by the practical point of view so, helplessly, he attacks Cross's wealth. What's it for? And again, Cross has the American answer, "The future, Mr. Gittes—the future." He is a grand political designer who doesn't have to bother to run for office. That is part of the American future, too. Is he a scoundrel, the sort of guy who was killed or brought to justice in 1937 films or who had the unlikely crisis of conscience that afflicts Senator Paine (Claude Rains) in *Mr. Smith Goes to Washington* (1939)?

Not quite? "I don't blame myself. You see, Mr. Gittes, most people never have to face the fact that at the right time and the right place, they're capable of anything."

There it is, the cold poison of reality to rot those homilies about bad guys getting their just deserts. It is the movie wisdom of 1974, when water implied Watergate, and it was written by Robert Towne. But a little against his will. Towne had wanted a happier ending, until the director, Roman Polanski, said no, it had to be as tough as life. And just as Polanski redid the ending, so it was the tiny thug he played who slit Nicholson's nose. But Polanski had had a life of damage in Poland—and there was more in L.A., much more, on Cielo Drive and then in Jack's own house.

Towne also dreamed of a Jake Gittes trilogy—the 30s, the 40s, the 50s, the history of water and oil, of public transport and the automobile. But that never came to pass either. People like Cross were truly in charge by then. And the code of Philip Marlowe was a dusty relic.

"...most people never have to face the fact that... they're capable of anything."

228

THE PASSENGER

1975, MICHELANGELO ANTONIONI

Through the Window

I am doing my best, but the more richly cinematic a moment on-screen, the harder it is to describe, and perhaps the more futile. You have to see these films; you have to be present. So you have to see Michelangelo Antonioni's *The Passenger*, and preferably on a large screen, as large as its window.

David Locke (Jack Nicholson) is an esteemed foreign correspondent deep in the African desert. Frustrated with his assignment, and much more, he swaps identity with a man named Robertson who dies in the hotel they share. Thus Locke gives up his wife, his London home and his job and starts to keep the appointments in Robertson's diary. These turn out to be part of the weapons-supply business. As he travels, he picks up an unnamed girl (Maria Schneider).

OPPOSITE: *In Antonioni films, buildings often frame characters and trap them—then you add color.*

But his wife and his television producer are suspicious. She wants to find Robertson who may know what happened to Locke. The pursuit, or the journey, goes by way of Germany to Barcelona and then farther south in Spain. At last, running out of energy or will, Locke and the girl arrive at the Hotel de la Gloria, where Robertson had an appointment.

Locke's room has the window I referred to. He lies down on the bed and asks the girl to leave him. She goes next door. And then the camera begins to track very slowly toward the window. As it sees more, we see and hear the late-afternoon passage of listless reality—some passersby, a dog, a taxi. Then a car pulls up and two men get out. We have seen them already in the film and we guess they have come for Robertson or Locke. They gaze at the hotel. A Spanish girl passes by, and the two men watch her.

As the camera gets closer to the barred window, we hear what might be a knock on the door in the room behind us. There are other noises—a scuffle? Is it a shot? And then the camera comes to the barrier of the bars—it might be a screen or the frontier between fiction and reality—and it passes through. It does the seemingly impossible with a sense of liberation and uplift.

In the dusty yard outside the camera sees a police car arriving. Locke's wife is with the policemen. The girl is in the courtyard. They all go back into the hotel and the camera turns a half circle to reveal the room it has left, with the bars in place. Locke is on the bed but he appears to be dead now. This is confirmed by the police when they enter the room. They ask the wife, does she recognize him. "I never knew him," she answers. But the girl says she knew him.

"… the camera comes to the barrier of the bars— it might be a screen or the frontier between fiction and reality—and it passes through."

"You can say the film is a mystery or a stream of consciousness."

The sense of escape or uplift may have occurred just as Locke died. Of course, the bars on the windows could be slid in and out. I think we know that, but I don't think it detracts from the magical effect of the camera movement or the tranquil air with which the story is resolved. You can say that Locke's ennui snuffed him out finally, or that he found the necessary vehicle for his own crossing of the frontier. You can argue as to whether the girl is a fond, chance encounter (though there is a striking coincidence in the way she appears) or part of the conspiracy that involves Africa and gunrunning. You can say the film is a mystery or a stream of consciousness.

You have to remember that disappearance is a subject close to Antonioni's heart—in *L'Avventura* (1960), one character vanished and never came back.

The Passenger was not a great success when it first appeared (its survival owed a good deal to Jack Nicholson's affection for the picture). You can see it on DVD or television—you may have to—but there is a real feeling in theaters that that last hotel room is like the room we once called a cinema. It is one of the most beautiful and unfathomable moving shots in the history of film.

TAXI DRIVER

1976, MARTIN SCORSESE

The Imagined Allure of Violence

I t was said at the time of its opening, with absolute justice, that *Taxi Driver* stood for so many good things in the new American cinema, not least the intense, fraternal collaboration of Martin Scorsese, Robert De Niro (the film's Travis Bickle) and the screenwriter, Paul Schrader. Still, for all that glorious teamwork, there are different strands within the film, and thirty-five years later the three careers have moved off in their own directions, which is not to say that their friendship has been compromised. A case can be made with all three that this was the best or the most startling thing they ever did. It's a film crammed with moments, or elements. Nearly every scene has always seemed original and raw; and no one should forget the wounded color scheme by Michael Chapman or Bernard Herrmann's last score.

But I'm picking on two scenes that seem to me to have an affinity: I don't know if I can explain it satisfactorily, but in both of them Travis is driving the cab.

First of all, at night on Park Avenue, he picks up a passenger who orders him to go to 417 Central Park West. When they arrive, the man says, "Just sit there." He wants to look at a second-floor window and the figure of a woman. He tells Travis it's his wife. She's having an affair, and he's going to kill her. With a .44 Magnum pistol. He's quite clear about what he's going to do. "Did you ever see what a .44 Magnum pistol will do to a woman's face? . . . Did you ever see what it can do to a woman's pussy?"

Nothing of this happens. The man stays in the back seat while Travis watches him in the rearview mirror. And in Schrader's script (published by Faber in 1990)

Martin Scorsese as a backseat driver.
Robert De Niro as the Taxi Driver.

there is this direction: "Camera closes in on Travis's face: He is watching the woman in the seventh-floor [sic] window with complete and total absorption. It's the same glazed-over stare we saw in his eyes as he watched the porno movie."

That refers to the earlier scene where Travis took Betsy (Cybill Shepherd) to an X-rated movie and lost any chance with her. It's a literary link, because I don't think it's really felt on the screen. But it's Schrader's notion of the association between pornography and violence (spelled out in his own later film *Hardcore*). One reason why we don't pick up on that reference is because—like Travis—we are so riveted by the passenger, who happens to be played by

Scorsese himself, a tiny demon with a black beard. He took the part at the last minute and he is scalding, brilliant and dangerous. But he is the scene. Travis becomes the passenger, and we are left to ask ourselves how far the seething dialogue is a real threat or mere language, a diversionary fantasy being acted out. In that sense, it helps us see how far *Taxi Driver* is a film about the imaginary allure of violence as much as the real impact. It's about movie violence.

Now come forward to the end where Travis, after the slaughter he has committed (three dead), and after his own recovery, is a cabbie again and by chance he picks up Betsy. She is more impressed with him than she has ever been. He is a kind of dark celebrity. The violence she heard about has changed her attitude, though you might argue that Bickle's madness was proved by what he did. But he is at liberty and oddly empowered: He gives her a free ride and she says maybe she'll see him again. Is that just a casual remark? He seems to dismiss it. But will she ever forget him and the way in which his outburst has made him a hero? I think a lot of these ideas come from Schrader. But the intensity of these moments belongs to Scorsese and his immense fascination with violence—which doesn't mean he likes it, but he wants to act it out. And he has never really been able to stop looking at it. The struggle between the two comes to a head in the pale, tortured devil-saint that De Niro made of Travis, a figure that owes something to Robert Bresson and as much to the director's childhood fears growing up in Little Italy.

"... will she ever forget him and the way in which his outburst has made him a hero?"

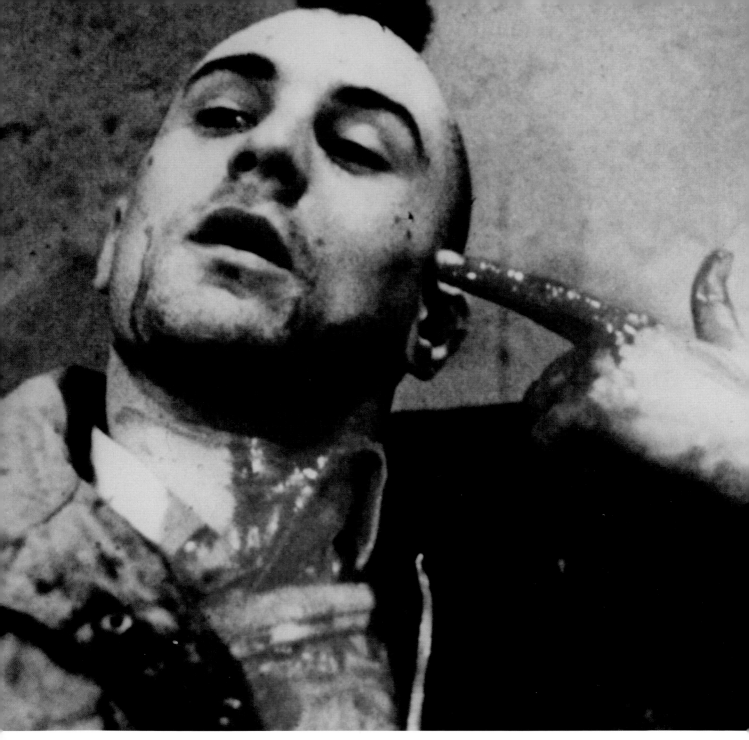

Are you looking at me? Travis Bickle asking if the cops will shoot him.

THE SHINING

1980, STANLEY KUBRICK

Just One Drink

Jack Torrance (Jack Nicholson) has everything he wants—but it's not quite enough. There he is, with his wife Wendy (Shelley Duvall) and his little boy Danny (Danny Lloyd), caretaking the Overlook Hotel for the winter. Perfect—unless you think the whole job could be a setup or a trap. The Overlook is up in the Colorado Rockies, in what most people might regard as ideal winter sports country—there is going to a be a ton of snow before this is over. So why is it closed? The hotel people say, Oh, it's far too expensive to keep it running in the winter, so it's just a summer resort. Like sharks off the coast of Massachusetts? Anyway, why complain? This is the way it was in the Stephen King novel, and it's a hell of a movie.

So the Torrances have a nice cozy apartment, and all the food they could eat from the hotel kitchen and its deep freeze. It's true, Danny isn't going to have any schooling, but at last Jack will really begin to get into the novel he's dreamed of. You may have known people who've kept telling themselves they're going to write a novel, and you know they're trouble. But Jack is a reformed character: it's true he did drink a little too much (in the past), and there were a few violent incidents. But if a guy's got a novel deep inside him it may be fighting to get out.

Jack Nicholson and Joe Turkel (as Lloyd the bartender).

Well, the writing isn't going too well, and Wendy can be a bit of a trial. What Jack would really like—if magic existed—is just one drink. A feature of the hotel is the Gold Bar. It's a magnificent place. We've seen it at the beginning and the light shines on the bar counter and all the bottles of liquor. You can picture the convivial crowd there on a summer evening. But in the winter the liquor goes to sleep and the bar is abandoned. Until one disconsolate day Jack is wandering through the empty acreage of the hotel and he sees the Gold Bar and thinks he'll just sit down at the counter and sort of get the feeling. An author needs to do research.

He covers his unshaved face and his depressed eyes with his hands and then he takes the hands away. What do you think? Wishing can work, because there is the tall, saturnine, slightly ghostly figure of Lloyd, the eternal barman, in the guise of Joe Turkel, an actor beloved of the director Stanley Kubrick, and deservedly so. "What'll it be?" whispers Lloyd.

The script is by Kubrick and the novelist Diane Johnson, and the chat here is absolutely neutral and regular—just the sort of stuff you might expect in a real bar—but we know we are at the entrance to the inner Overlook (not a bad title for a film book, by the way) in which the shine of the bar and its lights is preparation for the process of shining that can take you over the frontier and into another life, where the beast in you can roam. So the bar counter is one more version of the idea of a screen, with Lloyd welcoming you in. Jack begins to come to life: Why write a novel when you can live it out? He admits his problem with his family. He resumes his old addictions. And Lloyd is just as polite as a barman or an undertaker.

The Overlook Hotel in winter.

Things are going to get much more gruesome and when the winter blizzards come it will be so cold. The Overlook doesn't exactly shut down for the winter, and it only puts on an act in the summer. It gets down to its real business in the empty months, and that is "red rum" as read in a mirror—and while you're testing that out for yourself, you might care to have a little drink. Just snap your fingers and Lloyd will be with you. But take a careful look at him—is he actually alive or is it your imagination?

THE RIGHT STUFF

1983, PHILIP KAUFMAN

The Cowboy and the X-1

*T*he Right Stuff works on many levels, and perhaps that's what made its commercial life difficult. Or was it the awkward way in which the film's John Glenn (Ed Harris) seemed a "mistake" when set beside the very dull but contemporaneous campaigning of the real Senator Glenn?

It is a satire on heroism, hype and even space. Yet it believes in all those things and relishes them. Philip Kaufman, who directed and who did the screenplay from Tom Wolfe's book, has a genuine admiration for nerve and courage, yet he could see how far those things were being merchandised and

Sam Shepard goes riding in the desert as Chuck Yeager.

exploited already by the government. He loves flying, and the blue–black edge of space, yet I suspect he would agree (now at least) that the investment in the US space program might have been more sensibly applied on earth. Above all, this is a satire that is filled with beauty—and it may be that a lot of us find those two approaches hard to reconcile.

Here is beauty. Early on in the film, the test pilot Chuck Yeager (Sam Shepard) goes riding in the desert. The film's locations were in the area of Edwards Air Force Base in the Mojave Desert where many of the first test flights occurred. In life, Yeager (he's in the film, pushing himself at the camera!) was small, cheeky and mischievous. Whereas Shepard was chosen for his iconic and laconic resemblance to Gary Cooper and stars of that stature, as much as for his acting ability. He was also a rider, and there's something that harks back to the Western in the way he seems at liberty and fulfilled on horseback—it's so much more physical than being Spam in a can at Mach 1. But as this Yeager comes riding over a dune he hears and sees the X-1 itself, the crucial test plane, painted brick red, throbbing and steaming like a devil.

A man and an aircraft.

The symbolism is not stressed too much, but there we are in 1947 (in that sound barrier past) and it's the classic cowboy in a leather jacket coming face-to-face with modern technology. There's a lovely comparison in this part of the film between the desert and the heavens. They are different colors but they are equally awesome, infinite and in their way empty. Yet the small figures of men are challenged to explore them. We will see columns of smoke where aircraft crash in the desert, and there are cemeteries in the sand where the pilots are buried. There is also the shanty of a bar where the men drink and talk in the awful heat, and it is like the ideal saloon from a Western.

This film was made nearly thirty years ago and its resonance has only grown since then, as the operations of government and publicity have taken over increasing amounts of America and Americana. The "right stuff" has been drained away into "mission accomplished," another line from an actor in a leather jacket. The country may have lost confidence in its own stuff as the assertions about being the greatest of all nations have become more strident or redundant. That's why the humor in *The Right Stuff* is so precious. These heroes refuse to take themselves too seriously. In that sense, it's a film that reprises the mystique and perhaps even the reality of wartime flying films. And yet, we have to remember Joseph Heller's *Catch-22*, the book not the film, and then we may begin to wonder whether the "right stuff" was always more of a hope and a dream. But that leaves Kaufman's action film uncommonly wistful and gentle. I suspect it will look better still in time, if our stuff lasts.

"... the classic cowboy in a leather jacket coming face-to-face with modern technology."

The guys ready to go.
American heroes or
Spam in a can?

BLUE VELVET

1986, DAVID LYNCH

In Dreams

OPPOSITE:

The monster and the boy: Dennis Hopper and Kyle MacLachlan in Blue Velvet.

Imagine you have just walked in in the middle of the picture (as many of us used to do, and as the Surrealists, in the twenties, preferred to do). So, what do you see? We are in a nondescript room where the colors are those of flesh: pink and brown. We might be inside a body. Jeffrey (Kyle MacLachlan), who seems like a very nice boy and a very good boy is the prisoner of Frank (Dennis Hopper), his hair greased back, his leather jacket shiny, his mouth full of "Fuck!" his face so noble and angry. This seems to be Ben's place, and Ben (Dean Stockwell) is somewhere between suave and swish: He wears a ruffled shirt and a brocade jacket; he uses makeup and has a ring in one ear; and he speaks very softly. Frank urges Ben into a beer toast, a toast to their "Fuck." Meekly, Ben accedes. He is a gent. And a clip on the jaw from Frank makes Jeffrey part of it, too. Meanwhile, there is this desperate-looking woman, Dorothy (Isabella Rossellini), in a long blue velvet dress, waiting as if her life depended on it for something. Ah, it is the chance to see her child, in an inner room. She is admitted and through the door we hear her speaking to the child,

Flesh tones, the soft pink of walls and floor and the melodrama of blue.

Ben (Dean Stockwell) mimes "In Dreams."

assuring him that Mother loves him. There are a few other loutish men who stare and leer at Jeffrey—potential bullies—and there are some humdrum, middle-aged women, slatternly and past caring, who seem to be stale "girls." It is a nightmare. Brad Dourif in a silver lamé jacket is standing on the winged arm of a beat-up sofa. Don't ask why. Just let it pour out.

Carrying his cigarette holder, Ben sidles over to Jeffrey and thanks him for the toast—"It was very nice"—and then he punches Jeffrey with languid force in the stomach. The good boy doubles over.

Ben then gives Frank what I'm afraid may be drugs. They talk about the "sandman," and Jeffrey tries to overhear—this may be a clue! He is a boy detective as well as a kid looking into an inexplicable hell. And then Ben picks up a microphone that has a light in it that exaggerates the suave blankness of his face, and he begins to mime to Roy Orbison's "In Dreams." Some of the people in the room sway in what might be dance, but Frank is driven to a pitch of ecstatic anguish by the soulful song and its message. He mouths the words like a child. He is nearly weeping and he is compelled to stop the record player. Whereupon he rallies his psychic strength and roars out, "Let's hit the road! . . . Let's fuck!"

And so the helter-skelter moves on and the boy detective is drawn deeper into night town, with the clinging Dorothy, his mother, his lover, his disease, his adulthood. This is David Lynch's *Blue Velvet*, and it has a story that all gets tidied up in the end, though your faith in tidiness may be in need of treatment by then. It's best to drive with the moment I've described (Lynch loves transport and roads), to yield to its amazing on-screen conviction and beauty.

Beauty? Some of you are aghast. With all that torture and "Fuck!" stuff? In 1986 there were sober and reasonable critics outraged by the film. They thought it had gone too far. But it takes an outraged person to miss the weird lyricism or the surreal suitability of its adjacencies; and it takes a brave innocent to resist the film's insidious mining of our deepest psychic insecurities. This is just about seventy years after *The Birth of a Nation*, and the two films are like a Francis Bacon interior (is that where the colors come from?) side by side with a New England quilt from the 1870s. *Blue Velvet* is a great new film, still, just like *Citizen Kane*. But don't underestimate the tightly controlled dementia in those quilts or the long winters of repression and loneliness that made them.

Blue Velvet
shocked the world in 1986 but it is a fairy story about a boy and a girl, a witch and a beast.

"And so the helter-skelter moves on. . ."

WHEN HARRY MET SALLY...

1989, ROB REINER

The Soul of Schtick

Harry (Billy Crystal) wants Sally.

F rom the moment this book dawned, I guessed I would have to go back to Harry and Sally. Not that I found them so deserving; the big moments don't always come in outstanding pictures. Still, when I outlined the book, acquaintances knew I had to do *When Harry Met Sally*. They would feel wronged if I left it out.

On reviewing, it's less and more than I remembered. In 1989, Meg Ryan was pert, pretty, boyish, sexy. But now, I feel how vulnerable she seems, or scared. Not that that is due to the Billy Crystal character or Rob Reiner's direction, both of whom seem kind men. It's her being out in the open, watched or exposed. That brings her close to panic.

But Ryan was not a novice. She was twenty-seven when the film opened. Jean Harlow died a year younger. Ryan had made several pictures, with a broad, sketchy gesture toward "character" in *Top Gun*. She had met Dennis Quaid. She was the daughter of a casting agent, so she can hardly have been raised naïve.

There was a knowing edge to her even in 1989, and it fits with the attitudes of Reiner and screenwriter Nora Ephron who probably reckoned to make a Woody Allen picture, yet warmer and nicer. Harry and Sally are less characters than opportunities for players to smooch and banter. That's a method that worked well enough with William Powell and Myrna Loy. Sally is—or was—a modern girl, self-sufficient if romantic, able to look after herself, smart, sassy, independent. But scared. I don't know how far Ephron and Reiner meant that. Was it simply an inner wind in Meg Ryan's soul?

Now that Meg Ryan is fifty, after the break-up of her marriage, after soft focus has crept over her image to protect prettiness, and after the cruel dismissal of her more searching film, *In the Cut*, you feel for her.

Harry and Sally are in a Manhattan delicatessen, and their skirmish of the sexes turns on whether women sometimes fake sexual bliss to keep foolish men happy. The assumption is that Sally has had her share of experience, without being a tramp. So she'll just show the cocksure Harry. But Crystal (forty-two at the time) was and remains a child man. The scene would be impossible with, say, William Holden or even George Clooney.

OPPOSITE: *Sally wants a sandwich. The deli as a place of delight.*

251

"...pretending is sweeter than living."

So Sally fakes a momentous coming there in the deli. Ms. Ryan confessed at the time that it was an ordeal, even on a friendly set, and I don't think we should ask whether a "real" Sally would do this. We are in the realm of schtick—which can be a merry place, where players throw us a sweet wink to say, "Come on, we're all in this together."

There is a tension between Sally's boldness and Ryan's shyness. It's one thing to pretend to die on screen, but "coming" is tougher. Such a task would never have been assigned to Myrna Loy. You can't imagine Kim Novak faking an orgasm in *Vertigo* (though her character fakes nearly everything). That's why Ryan's timing is perfect. Her breathing so strenuous, her arc so brave yet predictable: We are watching a gymnast do a complicated set of floor exercises. And through it all there emerges the suspicion that Sally—let's stop there—has maybe never had an orgasm in her pert, pretty life.

You see, it's part of the soul of schtick, and of so many of our movies, that pretending is sweeter than living. After a hundred years of film, maybe, we have a population, very hip yet pretty inexperienced, that has seen so many wild, outrageous things on screens that it sort of knows how to do them. It knows how to fake it, and to act. But beneath that there is a tempest of behaviors that perhaps we never get to. You wonder, if Harry and Sally get married, will they produce children or a hit TV sitcom?

Of course, the first time you see the deli scene, you're stunned by the nerve and the fun in a public place. That's the arc that has the perfect topper and get-off line—"I'll have what she's having"—delivered by Rob Reiner's mother (the wife of a considerable comedy writer).

But if you study the scene separately, your gaze turns to how the trick is done and why. That's when you confront the inner wall that is a fear of sex or a feeling that that territory can never be entered. That's when the pathos of Meg Ryan lifts the scene out of 1989.

When Harry Met Sally was a hit, and the deli scene has entered into our daft diet. Meg Ryan was, if you like, lucky that she got to do that scene, though its pressure on her own reserve may have been vital to its effect. But that's why the slower, wounded gravity of a woman on her way to failure in *In The Cut* is the real thing and reason to honor her.

"I'll have what she's having."

OPPOSITE: *A key moment in sexual glory (and doubt), Sally and Meg Ryan go for it.*

HOFFA

1992, DANNY DEVITO

"I Know Who You Are"

Against the orders of the then leadership of the Teamsters union, the rebellious and charismatic Jimmy Hoffa (Jack Nicholson) heads a night march at the RTA company premises that results in appalling violence. In the gathering storm, he has a brief conversation with a young woman (Karen Young) who is carrying her child, a little boy, in her arms. This couple are not quite "right" for the occasion. It is a night for the men and their billy clubs. But the union speaks for the people, and this mother and child are as epic and emblematic as a similar couple in an early Soviet film, *Battleship Potemkin*. This is part of the unhindered emotional historicism of Danny De Vito's still-neglected film (as written by David Mamet).

The woman is tough, blunt and working class, even if Karen Young was a pretty actress who played some interesting lead roles. She was a familiar face in 1992, but her character goes unnamed. Nor will she tell Hoffa her son's name—"They are all called

Karen Young and Jack Nicholson.

something, aren't they?" she says. But when Hoffa tells her who he is, she comes back, tough but admiring: "I know who you are." This could be the knowledge of mere fame, from a woman who likely comes from a Teamster family. Why else is she there at this dangerous and unlikely event? Unless she is there to confront Hoffa and the whole movie? This is a movie (flexible with real history), but just because it's Karen Young and Jack Nicholson, looking at one another as equals, two great faces, we cannot rule out the possibility that they have known each other before and that she remembers this better than he does. Nothing supports this except the nature of film and looking, our curiosity, and the way she is there like a question mark.

Then the battle comes, brutal, bloody and often filmed from high angles

in sweeping camera shots. Mother and child are separated in the melee. She cries out to him—his name is Joey. The mother seems to disappear. Then the film dissolves from top-shot coverage of the battle to a high-angle tracking shot that reveals the several Teamster coffins from the struggle. We are at a collective funeral. Hoffa is sitting in the front row of the mourners beside his wife, who is as brazen blonde and empty as Karen Young is ashen and riveting.

But as Hoffa looks around the gathering, he realizes the young mother is not here—this is done on Nicholson's beady gaze, a mix of harshness and sentimentality. He spies the boy, sitting forlorn and alone, beneath his floppy man's cap. The mother is not there. The worry in Hoffa leads us into grief or fear, yet we still don't know whether he cares for anyone, or for this woman. A sense of incipient tragedy builds.

Hoffa gets up and walks slowly through the congregation. A plate of food appears beside the boy—it is his mother giving it to him. Hoffa exchanges one

glance with the woman. He tries to smile. She doesn't bother. He is the instrument of history but she is history itself. He has had a defeat that cunning will turn into victory and criminal alliance. She has seen violence, terror and damage. She could be her own ghost (much of *Hoffa* is poised between realism and dream).

They pass by without a touch or a kiss or another look. But in its way this moment has embodied the virtue of Hoffa—his generosity, his socialism, his need to care for ordinary people—as much as his compromise, his deviousness and his indifference to individuals. Have the two of them been lovers in some past? The lengthy film doesn't have such a scene. But its possibility has been planted with a restraint that builds the mystery in the whole film. Hoffa was a bad man? Easily agreed. He was a force for good and improvement? Cannot be denied. Was there once an American film that balanced such ambiguity?

"Was there once an American film that balanced such ambiguity?"

ONE FALSE MOVE

1992, CARL FRANKLIN

Living a Dream

One night in Los Angeles, two men and a woman stage a drug heist that leaves six people dead. They are Pluto, Ray, and an attractive, weak girl named Fantasia. When the police arrive, they find a fragment of camcorder video that names Fantasia and suggests she has a connection with Star City, Arkansas. The cops reason that the trio may be headed there. Two cops set off for Star City, having alerted the small town's police chief, Dale Dixon. In his way, Dale is another Fantasia—he lives in a dream of doing important, exciting police work. So the prospect of this big L.A. case arouses him and turns him into a talking machine.

The L.A. cops, Dud Cole and John McFeely, find Dale amusing—his nickname in the town is "Hurricane"—but they go along with his zealous help, though Dale's wife knows that her husband's overeagerness could get him killed. At one point, Dale, carried away by the whole thing, asks Dud if maybe he could come to L.A. and join that police force and work with them.

Meanwhile, the three outlaws are moving through Texas. In Houston, trying to sell their drugs, they kill their connections. They stop at a convenience store where a surveillance camera records Ray and Fantasia. A cop follows them, pulls them over, and it is Fantasia who shoots him dead.

Then we go back to the diner in Star City where Dud is telling John about Dale's suggestion. They chuckle over it, in good nature—they are not bad men—but Dale overhears them. And all the wind is taken out of his sails.

The cops realize this and they feel badly, even though Dale needs to face facts. But reality is a shotgun with two barrels. At that moment they receive a printout of the convenience store footage, and Dale is devastated again, yet more mysteriously. The "Fantasia" in the picture, he says, is actually Lila Walker. She used to live in Star City and Dale knew her. "Lila" is mother to a five-year-old who lives in town with grandparents. She could be coming back to see him. At all this news, Dale slumps in a chair by a window looking out on the green country. The city cops realize that there is more to Dale than they guessed.

"...reality is a shotgun with two barrels."

Bill Paxton as Dale Dixon

This is how *One False Move* goes from its hideous opening violence into a subtle study of dismay and race. Pluto is black, so is McFeely. Fantasia is of mixed blood: She had a white father, and so did her son. The script for the film was written by Tom Epperson and Billy Bob Thornton (who plays Ray), and the film was directed by Carl Franklin. The movie was reckoned in advance as something that would go straight to video, but the result was so tense and so interesting about people that it got the theatrical release it deserved.

The story ends with violence, just as it began, and it's a touch too tidy in its resolution. But the writing, the direction, and the acting transcend those limits. Dale and Fantasia are two people bound together by a faith in story rescuing dull lives: She wanted to be a movie star; he wants to be an L.A. cop like the ones on television. But in that commitment to dream they may have fathered an orphan.

Cynda Williams
and Bill Paxton

Franklin is a fine director: He would go on to make *One True Thing* and *Out of Time*, but since then he has worked in television. Can you guess what color he is? Dale is played by Bill Paxton. Pluto is Michael Beach, Fantasia is Cynda Williams, Dud and John are Jim Metzler and Earl Billings. Williams made other films, but nothing that developed her promise in *One False Move*. She is forty-six now, and around the time of the film she was married to Billy Bob Thornton. Bill Paxton works steadily, and he has good parts in *Apollo 13* and *Twister*. He is fifty-seven. Billy Bob Thornton won an Oscar for writing *Sling Blade*, and he was nominated for his acting in the same film. Billy Bob is famous still, but he hasn't made a good film for too long. What I'm trying to suggest is that the movie world is full of Dale Dixons, and sometimes years later they look back on a moment like *One False Move* and realize that that then was their brief now.

HEAT

1995, MICHAEL MANN

Meeting Cute

More than twenty years after playing father and son, Robert De Niro and Al Pacino faced the prospect of acting together in Michael Mann's *Heat*. They had both appeared in *The Godfather Part II*, but without sharing a scene. So just as Friedrich Schiller knew that if he had Mary, Queen of Scots and Queen Elizabeth I in the same play, it was unsporting to deny them a meeting (despite that event being absent from history), so everyone knew that the cop, Vincent Hanna (Pacino), and the gangster, Neil McCauley (De Niro), had to meet. And meet cute—at least at the level of cuteness that applies to actors playing hard men.

Neil is planning a big takedown. Vincent knows this, but doesn't know enough to stop it. And in truth he wants it to happen, because he wants a showdown, and because he's a cop in a movie that needs a climax. So, at a certain point in the film, when he knows Neil is driving alone on a freeway, Vincent arranges a helicopter to drop him on the road so he can pick up a car, pull Neil over, and suggest they have a cup of coffee. It's an expensive cup, but they're in a movie that cost $60 million.

Cut to the coffee shop and the confrontation. In his British Film Institute book on *Heat*, Nick James reports the legend that De Niro and Pacino actually did their filming separately, and what follows textually is a series of cross-cut close-ups or over-the-shoulder shots where it might be a sit-in whose back of the head we can see. So it might have happened. But James reports production stills that show the two men together, and I find it hard to believe that these warriors could resist the contest and the inescapable sentimentality. It may have been Michael Mann who kept a stylistic auster-ity that left the question open.

In any conventional, mano a mano sense, it's great value for money, though it's true that the writing and the situation favor Neil (he's trapped, more vulnerable, more dangerous) and so it's no surprise that (in my estima-tion) De Niro wins the scene. There is some comfort in this for it suggests that he was still a great actor despite the long and ongoing series of bad movies he had been doing. He makes Pacino look a little bit of a showboat, and I think De Niro knows it and rubs it in.

"What a scene it might have been…"

But that's not all. *Heat* has many claims to spectacular realism, not just in its violence and its acting, but in its use of real Los Angeles locations and in its hard-boiled or cynical assumption that, in truth, cops and robbers are rather alike. Don't they put themselves on the line on the same streets with the same weapons and a similar code of honor? The two men share a lot of terse talk to that effect. Choice seems to have collapsed. "I don't know how to do anything else," says Vincent. "Neither do I," agrees Neil. There is a grin of complicity.

But do we really believe this? The cops are there to defend law and order, and us; the gangsters mean to defy it. Have you ever been a victim of crime, or a bystander caught up in it? Did you feel the cops and the hoods were the same? If Neil succeeds in his job he will probably take down in person in an hour ten times what Vincent could earn in a year. So the fact that the two men are both stylishly dressed and sharing coffee and tough talk is a trick, a fancy. It is a gross sentimentality of the movies that these two men are alike. In crucial ways in life they are opposites. But the movie lie has sunk in now, and it's hard to erase.

So this is a great moment, if you like, in a picture shot by one of the most expert filmmakers we possess. But its greatness is confined and hobbled by being "only a movie," based on pipe dream and dangerous mythmaking. What a scene it might have been if Vincent and Neil bumped into each other by chance but never recognized their official roles.

FOLLOWING PAGE: *In the romance of* Heat, *the cop and the crook are offered as mirror images.*

HEAT

263

THE PIANO TEACHER

2001, MICHAEL HANEKE

Double Concerto

For some time now, there have been uncomfortable films, movies that would sooner not exist than make us feel good. Though how we feel good is less easily defined these days: A woman with a sublime understanding of Schubert may step into her own empty bath and make razor cuts on her private parts, for relief. The mystery is always in the privacy.

Still, once upon a time, the movies accepted their duty of bringing comfort without demur. So there might have been a story of a piano teacher of a certain age, dedicated to the music, tormented by the difficult mother she has to look after, who meets a brilliant young male student and they do not just fall in love, they leap at it and collapse in a fond heap with a double concerto washing over their glory and happiness.

Erika Kohut (Isabelle Huppert) is brilliant, cold and desperate. Her mastery of Schubert is so much more than her self-control.

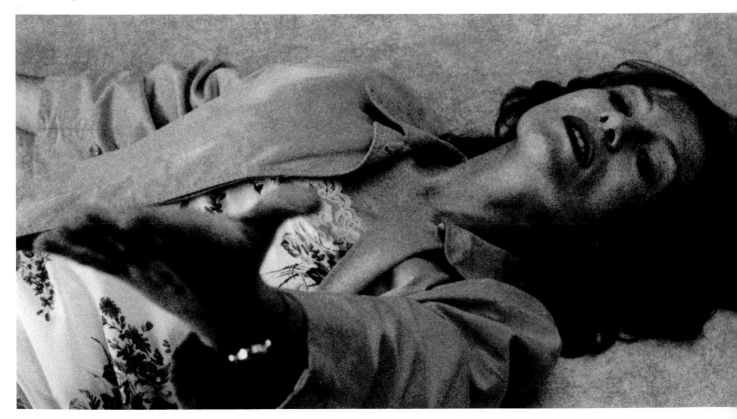

Erika Kohut (Isabelle Huppert) does not believe in that movie. She clings to a double life in which she is a strict arbiter of musical taste in Vienna, and a secret orgiast in sexual rites where pleasure has long since been excluded by controlling coldness, sadomasochism and self-abuse. Erika is as beautiful as Huppert—red-brown hair, freckles, a shifty mouth, trembling eyes—and as dangerous and nasty as this most audacious of actresses can make her.

There are so many moments to pick from: the razor in the bath; the meditative process that puts broken glass in the pocket of a female student who is simply friends with the boy whose infatuation Erika refuses with that blankest of faces, the face on the Metro (or whatever system you use) that is planning assassination and debauchery and waiting for her stop. There is the moment when Erika goes to see a hardcore pornographic movie and holds a white handkerchief to her mouth—like your aunt at a bullfight, or like a girl who may need to spit back imagination's cum.

None of those. Instead, there is the scene, at night, where Erika comes upon a drive-in movie. There is a screen in the scene, with movie moments going by like the cars on a freight train. Erika slips quietly on foot among the parked cars, until she hears the sounds of urgent lovemaking from one car. A boy and a girl are on the backseat, and we can hear that the girl is on the way to coming.

Erika is mesmerized: We have her watchful face—as sharp as a sniper in the real dark—and the glass window of the car (it is a film full of screens, both image-bearing and separating or hiding). She crouches down beside the back door of the car only a few feet from the fucking. Her hand goes inside her raincoat and she starts to masturbate to the inner scene. Did I mention that we are watching her, just as she is watching them?

But then, close to climax, the girl asks what's the matter. In his plunging action the boy's head has come up and he has noticed Erika. It stops his drive-in. He glares at her—of course, he could invite her in, but he's not a subtle boy—and with his pants hobbling his ankles, he tries to get out of the car and chase her.

"Erika is at the same time one of the great monsters in screen history, and a saint of self-destruction."

Erika does get away. There is more to come in her fearsome struggle between beauty and madness. Michael Haneke directed from the 1983 novel by Elfriede Jelinek. Erika is at the same time one of the great monsters in screen history, and a saint of self-destruction. Many viewers would say this is not for them—it is too ugly, too sordid, too unpleasant. They should be excused. The Grand Tour of Europe does not have to take in Auschwitz. But picking flowers and listening to Schubert will not take the camp away. Meantime, *The Piano Teacher* is as remorselessly beautiful as if Erika had made it. There can be no higher compliment or graver warning.

"Did I mention that we are watching her,
just as she is watching them?"

IN THE CUT

2003, JANE CAMPION

No False Glamour

Fourteen years have passed since *When Harry Met Sally.* When she played Frannie Avery in *In the Cut,* Meg Ryan was forty-two—a dangerous age in a film all about danger, not just that of being a woman alone in a city that has killers, but of committing to love and sex. Earlier in this book, I used *When Harry Met Sally* as a moment, and I may have hurt or disappointed you in dismantling a scene that is proverbial good fun in a film that was a hit. *In the Cut* was not a success, either at the box office or with critics. Indeed, it was attacked. I think it is a masterpiece, a tribute to the courage of the actress and the passion of her director, Jane Campion.

I find it hard to select moments, so I will cheat a little and pick two. But I have to treat them cautiously if I am not to spoil the story. There is a killer at work in New York. The head of a female victim is found in the garden to the building where Frannie lives. She is alone in life, save for her half sister (Jennifer Jason Leigh); she teaches English at a college. A detective comes to talk to her about the head—he is played by Mark Ruffalo. He is plainly tough, just as he is attracted to her. Later, she is mugged on the street and he comes to interview her again at her apartment. They make love; they have sex. She is drawn to him, yet she doesn't trust him. In part that is because she has a thought he could be the killer. But it is also the natural hesitation of a forty-two-year-old woman on the brink of love, or sex or maybe both.

Ryan looks forty-two and she uses nothing in the way of makeup to disguise this. She has a beautiful body and she strips for the detective and the camera. He performs cunnilingus on her and she is powerfully gratified. We see the man's penis, if briefly—but that is an important and rare item in movie sex. Campion films Frannie close-up from a distance so that her surroundings are often out of focus. That brings a tender, emotional feeling to the whole movie. It is not just that the sex is handled with rare openness. It is deeply touching, without ever quite dispelling the fear. Dread and desire are like two bodies in intercourse.

"Dread and desire are like two bodies in intercourse."

Cut. Much has happened. Two other women have been murdered. Frannie herself has had to kill someone. Then we see her barefoot in a gorgeous red dress, walking home on an empty highway. As well as the red dress, much of her body is tattooed with blood—she looks like someone who has been through an initiation rite. And then she comes to an overflowing green garden. It is her garden, and it is not the most plausible location in Manhattan maybe. But Campion has made *In the Cut* a sumptuous conflict of red and green, wonderfully photographed by Dion Beebe. She passes through the garden.

I'm not going to tell you any more, except to say that *In the Cut* is taken from a novel by Susanna Moore. The author, Jane Campion, and Nicole Kidman (serving as producer) worked on the screenplay. Kidman was to have played Frannie. But her divorce came at the crucial moment and left her distracted. That was the story. Kidman is a fine actress and I am sure she would have made something amazing as Frannie. But she would not quite possess

the rather battered beauty and direct sensuality that existed in Meg Ryan. So many films are about sex, or so they want you to believe. *When Harry Met Sally* is like that, and it's fun, but it's bogus. *In the Cut* is the real thing, frightening throughout, sensual, arousing and blunt. There is no false glamour, no prettification; no one is cute.

What damage the film's failure did to Ryan's confidence is beyond measure. She took a great risk, and it is important to stress the quality of the result and to get you to see a movie that has been unfairly written off. It is one of the great films of the twenty-first century, and of the hundred years of film that preceded it.

"… but perhaps he *is* out of the past?"

BIRTH

2004, JONATHAN GLAZER

Wagner Has to Be Thanked

Anna (Nicole Kidman) has been married to Sean. Then one day as he was jogging in the snow in Central Park, he dropped dead. She thought it took her ten years to recover from the loss, but then she believed she could remarry, to Joseph (Danny Huston). There is a party to celebrate their engagement. An old friend (Anne Heche) brings a present but changes her mind about it at the last moment. She buries the gift in the park and buys something else. But a little boy sees the act of burial. His name is Sean (Cameron Bright), and soon thereafter he comes to Anna and tells her he is her Sean, and that she should not marry Joseph. He is ten, of course, but perhaps he *is* out of the past?

Anna lives in a smart apartment just off the park with her mother (Lauren Bacall), her sister and her brother-in-law. There is a faintly oppressive sense that she is still being looked after. Perhaps the process of mourning has been unusually disturbing. You see, a part of Anna—the sensible part—knows that this whole thing is silly, that Sean is lying or dreaming. But another part, the damaged part, the self that lost Sean, is not so sure. So she doesn't dismiss the possibility. There is no hint that she is religious or inclined to spiritual notions, but the loss of the first Sean has not fully healed. So the second Sean troubles her, and this worries her family.

The boy Sean comes to the apartment—it is an attempt to get to the bottom of the mystery, to humor him, to tidy the matter up. The brother-in-law (Arliss Howard) takes a leading role in this but he discovers that the boy knows surprising things about the dead Sean.

OPPOSITE: *Sean (Cameron Bright) sees a gift being buried in the park.*

Anna's mother (Lauren Bacall) with Sean. Is she asking him if he knows how to whistle?

One evening, Sean is there just as Anna and Joseph are dressed to go out to a concert. The boy is told he must abandon the idea of having Anna, and on the spot he faints. Anna sees this as she goes out the door, and she carries it in her mind to the concert. Here is the moment.

The concert is in progress as they arrive. Joseph and Anna are allowed to go to their seats as the music plays the prelude to Wagner's *Die Walküre*. And then the film settles into an intense close-up of Anna that is silent save for the

Wagner. This is an occasion in this book where it is more necessary than usual for me to tell you that you must see the film. Why? Because I cannot describe it adequately. That may be my limits—though I can see the temptation to write a whole novel about Anna—but it is more because when any art is working in its essence it cannot be translated. You would not expect me to paint a picture from a piece of music, I hope. Or provide a sculpture that "captures" *Anna Karenina*.

As the Wagner builds, the camera closes in on Anna (Nicole Kidman).

So I can say that the most special and indelible and infinite effect in the movie is not made in a computer, it is a shot of the human face when something momentous is happening to that person. You could say that the pressure of the music, coupled with the anguish she feels over the boy Sean, topples Anna over some kind of edge. Or you could say that she agrees with herself that she needs to believe this story—so she will go sanely mad. Or she might be thinking of the shopping she needs to do tomorrow, or of why Joseph is such a dead weight in bed when they make love so that she begins to feel stifled. Perhaps she is wondering, as she has wondered before, whether Sean, her Sean, was always faithful to her.

It is not a matter of Nicole Kidman being an exceptional actress, or Jonathan Glazer a special director, though they deserve the utmost praise for their work here. But Wagner has to be thanked, along with the whole idea for the film (script by Jean-Claude Carrière and Milo Addica, with Glazer). But we are a vital part of the process, too, and it might work with another actress and another piece of music—Isabelle Huppert with Mahler? Some audiences might say this prolonged close-up is foolish, just looking at her for so long while nothing happens, just as others might complain, "I don't believe any woman would be so carried away." But the thing about the movies is whether or not we are carried away, and how we will be if we get back.

A HISTORY OF VIOLENCE

2005, DAVID CRONENBERG

The Most Intimate Rivalry

He was really Joey Cusack. Now that he's killed his brother, will he go back to Millbrook or take over the gang in Philly?

Here is another title that aspires to a summation of so many thousands of movies, and it is a film replete with moments of violence, albeit of a rather more conventional genre than David Cronenberg was accustomed to. For a couple of decades, he could see eruptions of the body and society that violated so many anatomical norms. He was on the borders of science fiction and horror, all the way up to *Spider*, and then he seemed to shift attention. It may have helped that this script was by another hand—it was written by Josh Olson and adapted from a graphic novel. Thus, Cronenberg began to discover the ordinary genres in filmmaking. Indeed, *A History of Violence* is in some ways a new version of Jacques Tourneur's *Out of the Past* (1947), that film where Robert Mitchum has gone into hiding from a bad love affair and a debt to Kirk Douglas, until chance discovers him working in a small town on Highway 395 in California.

In this film, Tom Stall (Viggo Mortensen) is living in the cozily named Millbrook, Indiana, where he operates a diner. He has a wife (Maria Bello) and kids and he is a respected and appreciated person in his world. Until the past comes calling and compels him to regain the violence that once was his existence, his job and his nature. Gangsters try to rob him; he disposes of them and becomes a local hero. Then an older, wiser and scarred hood visits (the demonic side of Ed Harris), and says Tom is really Joey Cusack, once a gangster in Philadelphia. On several occasions, Tom repels these visitors from the past, though he is changed in the process—we see that if only in the way he makes love to his wife and in the fact that his son is drawn into the violence. At last, he realizes that he must go back to Philadelphia to his brother, to settle accounts.

"*A History of Violence* is a sweeping title, but the film earns it . . ."

This is the moment, as he returns to the vast, walnut-dark house in that city of brotherly love where his lost soul mate, Richie (William Hurt), lives. It is a showdown, with Richie eloquent in his complaints about how Tom brought so much grief and grievance on him. Of course, you won't want me to explain it in detail, though if you have been to the movies seven times in your life you can guess what happens (and that is part of your history of

*William Hurt as
Richie Cusack.*

violence). The reason I love the scene is that it is a great exchange between brothers, for there is wounded love between them as well as the certainty that someone is going to die. I can never forget the way Hurt whines the name "Joey," and I think you might have to go back to great models—to Dostoyevsky, even—to catch the layers of tension, unease and sheer need between brothers.

Fraternity is a great subject in film—it's there in *The King of Marvin Gardens*, and I could have included *Raging Bull* (the bond between Robert De Niro and Joe Pesci was a thriller for years, yet close to hideous, too), *Winchester '73* and so many others, including Cronenberg's own *Dead Ringers* (1988) in which Jeremy Irons plays twin brothers, the repressed and the irrepressible. Why are brothers so much at each other's throat in films? Does this conflict really correspond with life, or is fraternity a way of dramatizing the gulf between good and evil, comedy and drama, in all of us? Is it the most intimate rivalry and murder?

Whatever the answer (and I realize that sisters have their share of delighted torment, too—and I should hope so), it is quite an achievement to have Viggo Mortensen (a good actor) dominate a film and then be challenged by William Hurt (a great actor, but maybe a difficult man). *A History of Violence* is a sweeping title, but the film earns it, and this is one of the few movies that really require a sequel. Until you realize that *The God-father* (an ultimate portrait of brotherly differences) may have answered many of those questions. If Tom's peaceful, happy life was stalled once, it may be set free now.

"Why are brothers so much at each other's throat in films?"

INFAMOUS

2006, DOUGLAS MCGRATH

Inexplicable Unease

There is a school of thought that says the progress of a film must be orderly and attractive; it must be an arc on which we can tell where we're going. That's a sound and useful principle until it's not, for just as intrinsic to the nature of film as one frame coming logically after the next, there is the possibility of outrage, violent conjunction, impossibility or mystery. Suppose you start with that.

Infamous is not *Capote*. It came a year later, and thus it is the second movie about Truman Capote. You may remember that Philip Seymour Hoffman won the Oscar in the first film, and it's entirely respectable and worth seeing. But the second film, written and directed by Douglas McGrath, is superior. As you may tell from this.

We are in a smart Manhattan night club in 1959. The excited crowd includes Truman Capote (Toby Jones) and his close friend Babe Paley (Sigourney Weaver). Then the MC makes an announcement: Here comes the singer of the evening, "Kitty Dean." The introduction and the applause are enough to suggest—this is the mid-1950s—she might be Patti Page or Doris Day, an authentic star. She appears in short blonde hair and an elaborate off-white gown; she looks very much like Gwyneth Paltrow; and she begins to sing, "What Is This Thing Called Love?" by Cole Porter.

Truman and Babe react as if they feel very lucky to be there hearing Kitty Dean, though I am bound to say—and I don't mean to be churlish—that the person looking like Gwyneth Paltrow is not the greatest singer I've ever heard (I could imagine Simon Cowell being quite brusque with her). Never mind, it's a great song and a special club; she wears a knockout gown and she does look like Gwyneth Paltrow.

But then some inexplicable unease begins to seep into her. Does she guess she is not singing too well, or is she somehow affected by the nature of the Cole Porter lyrics she is using—"You made my life an enchanted dream 'til somebody else came near."

She comes to a halt. The music subsides. The people at the club are dismayed and anguished. They don't expect a smooth performer like Kitty Dean to break down or crack up, or not in public. She puts her hand to her head,

"Infamous is not Capote."

"Truman and Babe react as if they feel very lucky to be there hearing Kitty Dean . . ."

as if faint, or feeling the pangs of memory. She tries to start again. She mutters a few phrases a cappella. And then she recovers herself and resumes the song. The band starts playing again. The audience is revived. Kitty Dean never comes back, and there is never a word offered about who she is or why she was waylaid in her own song.

Truman Capote (Toby Jones) and Babe Paley (Sigourney Weaver) at the club.

Infamous resumes with the story of Capote hearing about the murder of the Clutter family in Holcomb, Kansas, and going there to research, as he sets off on the journey that will end with the book *In Cold Blood*, published in 1966. Though there is one moment in the film where the loquacious, if not glib, Truman is suddenly at a loss for words until he recovers himself.

I'm not sure whether that is truly a link or a coincidence, for I don't think the odd breakdown in Kitty Dean's act actually needs to be rhymed later or explained. It is enough just to establish that anyone—a performer or a human being—can be sailing along and then suddenly the flow breaks. It could be the mind cracking. It could be the rather conventional question, "What is this thing called love?," taking on an unavoidable meaning or pain.

All I'm trying to suggest is that in life, you may be at what seems like a climax in your story—you are getting married, or a lover is telling you it's all over—when something "unconnected" happens that immediately becomes connected: A man falls out of a window; a car bursts into flame; it starts to rain. Movies do not often entertain those out-of-the way things, and that's why movies sometimes feel claustrophobically organized. Most films don't want rain, or won't trust the real thing. So they lay on sprinklers. And the rain looks fake but significant. That's a pity, and I like this opening to *Infamous* because McGrath never stoops to explaining it.

" ... anyone ... can be sailing along and then suddenly the flow breaks."

OPPOSITE: *"Kitty Dean."*

ZODIAC

2007, DAVID FINCHER

Criminal and Camera

Don't pursue this moment if you haven't seen *Zodiac* and you think you might like to. On the other hand, if you're not sure, read the piece. I'm going to talk about the film's ending, but the closure stays very open, so you won't feel the unsettling impact until you live through this slow, unwinding and disconcerting experience.

The Zodiac was a real serial killer, roaming across California from the late 1960s for over ten years. He was never captured, and never fully identified. But this is a movie about the way a few men—cops and journalists—became obsessed with the case. And in obsession there is seldom closure. Thus, in *The Searchers*, Ethan Edwards (John Wayne) cannot admit that the quest or the overwhelming burden are over.

The three searchers in *Zodiac* are a San Francisco detective, David Toschi (Mark Ruffalo), officially on the case, Paul Avery (Robert Downey Jr.), a crime writer on the *San Francisco Chronicle*, and Robert Graysmith (Jake Gyllenhaal), the paper's cartoonist, and the only one of the trio without an assignment. Avery succumbs to his own alcoholism and personal recklessness. Toschi is hamstrung by his mounting caseload over the years and the dense accumulation of evidence. There is every sign here, despite the insolent nerve of the Zodiac himself, that the longer a case goes on, the less likely it is that a decent cop can deal with the mountain of files or solve the case. But Graysmith is the amateur, the most obsessed, even if his hours and years on the case put his marriage and family in jeopardy. But as the movie suggests, Graysmith alone works out the identity of the killer.

This is where one has to mention David Fincher, the director of the film. Fincher is not an artist who really likes life, or people. He had done a serial killer before, in *Se7en*, where Kevin Spacey revels in the gloating evil genius who plays with everyone—including us. And *Zodiac* is constructed in such a way that we are led to believe Arthur Leigh Allen is the killer. At one point, Leigh is questioned by the police. Toschi admits that this is the most likely suspect. And then, in a glimpse of chilling ease and contempt, the actor, John Carroll Lynch, simply crosses his legs. It is breathtaking and a revelation that

*In murder movies,
a lot of time is spent
questioning suspects.*

the Zodiac himself has no more compelling motive than fun, or the idea of a
game. (Of course, the Zodiac was his own publicist because of several taunt-
ing letters he sent to the San Francisco newspapers. And in *Se7en*, the Spacey
character delights in sending messages to hook his pursuers.)

The interrogation of Leigh is one moment, but it only sets us up for the
greater mystery of the final confrontation. Graysmith believes he knows the
answer. He realizes that Leigh is working in a hardware store in Vallejo, a
town to the north of San Francisco—is it the first hardware store in a movie
since the Sam Loomis place in Fairvale in *Psycho*? Graysmith goes to Vallejo.

He enters the store and starts to look for Leigh. The camera is pushed back by his progress, and then we see a clerk at the counter. When he turns, it is Leigh, and like any helpful clerk he asks, "Can I help you?." Graysmith says nothing and then he says, "No," but by then Leigh has realized this is no ordinary customer. This is identification. This is game, set and match, and Leigh's expression goes from confusion through anxiety to a deathly command. He knows he is known, and he knows that Graysmith is not the police. But he realizes that his magnificent mystery is broken; his sublime game is over.

The moment is held long enough to reach beyond the conditions of a crime film. I mentioned *Psycho* in no casual way. Hitchcock was fascinated by the dynamic that exists between killer and detective, between criminal and camera, between the screen and us. So this moment in *Zodiac* makes me think of the instant in *Psycho* when we see that Anthony Perkins and John Gavin, Norman and Sam, are mirror images. Beyond that it reminds me of Raymond Burr in *Rear Window*, discovered at last, and asking Jimmy Stewart, "What do you want from me?"

I think that's what *Zodiac* amounts to, and what hangs in the air over this face-off. It's a question Fincher is asking of himself and us: What *do* we want of these terrible, violent movies, where murder itself can be raised to the level of art or the most dangerous game?

Jake Gyllenhaal as the man who is obsessed by his search.

Is this him? Is this the Zodiac? Arthur Leigh Allen played by John Carroll Lynch. The case was never solved.

When the film is over, small-type titles tell us many things, including the fact that Leigh died before arrest. But even then, the physical evidence cleared him. The case is inactive, but not closed. So the mystery comes back. Movie is so reluctant to dispatch its monsters.

"... Leigh's expression goes from confusion through anxiety to a deathly command."

BURN AFTER READING

2008, ETHAN COEN, JOEL COEN

Discreet Gems

It may say something about me that I'd rather not examine too closely; it may simply be a matter of the absence of taste. Yet I wonder if "taste" at the movies isn't a very suspect or ambivalent thing. I'm never sure I believe in it, and I know I don't want to be belabored with it or taught to have it. So while plenty of people feel amiably toward this film, they may be surprised to see it being picked out for special attention. Why be afraid of surprise? And why not look at this one again? I realize that even fans of the Coen Brothers will have several other films they'd place above this one—*No Country for Old Men, Miller's Crossing, Fargo, The Big Lebowski, A Serious Man*. Admirable choices, but I am not going to be deterred. *Burn After Reading* is one of the funniest films made this century.

I have to list its chief assets: Brad Pitt, giving every hint that comedy could be his thing; George Clooney, beginning to get into an exploration of how fake he is—surely his destiny as an actor if he is to avoid being another Robert Redford; Tilda Swinton, possessed by such secret, towering furies; Frances McDormand—enough said; Richard Jenkins, unlucky again; and, of

OPPOSITE ABOVE:
Brad Pitt in his funniest performance.

OPPOSITE BELOW:
George Clooney might be our Cary Grant if he played more comedy.

BELOW: *Frances McDormand suspects she's being watched.*

The comedy turns nasty as John Malkovich pursues Richard Jenkins.

course, John Malkovich, being deeply wronged—that really is the proper use of his unapologetic superiority. I could find moments among that group, and intricacies of plot that would take several hundred words to describe. But what I like most of all, and what goes to the heart of our obsession with "Intelligence" that defies its own name is the final scene involving two supporting actors—if you are still locked into that scheme of labeling.

They are David Rasche as a CIA officer and J. K. Simmons as his superior. We have seen them briefly earlier, but this set-piece scene is simply the officer reporting to the superior on how the chaos of the film has been cleared up, and the superior's weary knowledge that this entire CIA thing might be so much more manageable if there were no people. Human nature is always going to get in the way. The humor springs from Rasche and Simmons both playing the scene dead straight, and I can believe that much of the dialogue could have come from a real conference in that hallowed organization at Langley (if it's really there).

I like CIA films—I actually appreciate Robert De Niro's dogged *The Good Shepherd* quite a lot, and I would support a grant that would require him to make more films like that instead of acting. But such stories are very earnest and they know that the CIA can do and has done terrible damage in the name of making us more secure. Why on earth do people want to be secure? On the whole, I think that impacted secret organizations with a life and death of their own are fitter subjects for comedy, for Preston Sturges, Jacques Tati or the Coen Brothers. And I love the level of humorless satire in the Rasche-Simmons debriefing, and the solemnity with which such guardians of our well-being feel they should talk.

I could quote the dialogue, but I don't want to spoil it for you. I am already a little dismayed that Simmons's expertness in the picture helped get him the lead boss role in some amusing television commercials for Farmers Insurance. They're better than most ads, but they needed the Coen Brothers as well as a modest exposé of the principles of a benign insurance business. Still, I can hear the earnestness of Mr. Simmons talking about the necessity of work! He's fifty-five and he works his butt off doing TV because that's the only way he survives. (And David Rasche, who is older, was in *Rubicon*—enough said?) Never mind, sirs, in *Burn After Reading*, the two of you are discreet gems—even if you tempt me to suggest that the film (and the level of scholarship at the CIA) might have been more aptly described as "Burn Before Reading."

"Why on earth do people want to be secure?"

J.K. Simmons as the head of the CIA?

STILL PHOTOGRAPH, VANCOUVER, THE EVENING AFTER THE CANUCKS LOST THE STANLEY CUP

2011, RICHARD LAM

First or Last?

What's this, you say. How does a still picture get into this collection of movie moments? The answer is straightforward. A moment can be an instant and in its early life, and for a long time thereafter, a movie was twenty-four still frames a second agitated and given duration by projection. So movie is made of stills, and anyone who looked at this picture, and who was charmed and stopped by it—which was more or less everyone for a day or two—was struck by how movie-like it was. And in that association, we need to see that movie does not simply seem to move. It moves us, too.

So, on that day in June 2011, in Game 7 of the Stanley Cup, the Boston Bruins came to Vancouver and won 4–0. Against most early predictions, and the fact that the Vancouver Canucks had won the first two games of the series, Vancouver had been defeated. In the aftermath (it was early evening still on the West Coast) some disappointed fans, some opportunists and some by-passers had a riot. I don't mean to minimize it. There was damage, injuries and riot squads with helmets, shields and truncheons. It was big enough for press photographers.

Rich Lam of Getty Images was one of the photographers. He took a string of pictures and today that can be done with a camera set on automatic and taking in images as the cameraman points it, or does not aim, focus and frame. In a sense, it is a surveillance camera, interfered with by human agency. As it was, Mr. Lam would say later that he was hardly aware of what he had "taken" or recorded at the time. It was only later, as he checked through his files, that he saw the picture—and its wealth of meaning.

You know the picture—or you did for a few days. It has three planes or levels. In the foreground on the right there is the dark, blurred figure of a riot policeman, facing the camera and holding a stick. It's not clear if he knows the camera is there, or means to do anything about it. But the figure is suggestive of force and menace.

In the far plane, the third, also out of focus, we see a line of policemen with the public behind them and the amber flare of street lighting.

Then there is the middle plane, in perfect focus, so that we cannot miss the bare legs and the thighs of a young woman on her back on the street who is being kissed by a young man lying beside her. The first thought inspired by the picture is that some kids are ready to do it anywhere, even in the midst of a riot, and there is a natural tenderness not just in the body language of the couple, but in the curiosity that has spied them. Later on, the possibility arose that the girl had been hurt in the riot and the boy was comforting her. That's tender, too, but not as potent as the sheer innocence of the embrace.

It was an image as memorable and piercing (which doesn't mean we won't forget it) as Robert Capa's photograph of an infantryman in the Spanish Civil War being shot, or Robert Doisneau's photograph known as "The Kiss," an apparently spontaneous snapshot of two people on the streets of Paris in 1950. (Were they strangers, or lovers?)

Of course, those comparisons are warnings, too. It has been established that the Doisneau shot was preconceived and arranged. There is also a lot of suspicion that the Capa photograph could not have occurred in reality—it, too, was contrived. Nothing as yet suggests any such doubts about the picture from Vancouver. But the mere precision of focus does make us feel like an audience seeing a moment in a story or a movie—is it the first shot or the last? Did it happen like life? Or does photography itself so love the lifelike that it leaves provenance always uncertain? A photo is fact, isn't it, a record of light and where the light falls? It is real. But as soon as you look at a picture, you have crossed the threshold of fiction.

Welcome.

"... movie does not simply seem to move. It moves us, too."

The first shot of a movie, or the last?

INDEX

ACKNOWLEDGMENTS

There are books that go through writing and production in a routine way; there are some that prove to be a lot of fun. And then there is this one, over which there was a greater feeling of something coming to life than I have ever known before. Above all, I am grateful to Will Balliett, who helped form the initial idea and then gave it wings. Apologetic, hesitant, droll, hassled he is a master of all those styles, but they do not conceal his mastery, his dedication, his taste or his enthusiasm. He pushed me in many directions and he insisted, hesitantly, on the form of the book and the spectacular nature of illustrations that went beyond the genre of "film still."

At every step of the way, Elizabeth Keene (Will's assistant) was resourceful, quick, entertaining and brilliant, probably in far more ways than I know about. The design of the book is by Beth Tondreau, and it is beyond any dreams I had at the start of the project. I don't think there are many film books that have this quality and the vision belongs to Beth. She was ably assisted by Jennifer Berry as picture researcher and by Derek Davidson at PhotoFest.

In addition, I want to thank Rick Ball for copy-editing and Navorn Johnson for proof-reading. The marketing and publicity were handled by Lauren Miller, Harry Burton, Tiffany Alvarado McKenna and Kait Howard.

Finally, I want to pay tribute to the three women to whom this book is dedicated: Mary Corliss, Lucy Gray and Molly Haskell. I know that they, too, have done more than I know about. But I want to single out Mary for this reason: For decades she was the curator of the movie stills department at the Museum of Modern Art in New York. Nearly every writer on film benefited from her knowledge of the collection, her understanding of what worked and her ability to find it. She was a treasure at a treasury. But then MOMA took the decision of closing down its stills library, moving it to a remote place and dispensing with Mary's services. MOMA does many things wonderfully well, but it has its self-inflicted disasters. The look of this book is for Mary.

PHOTO CREDITS